Challenging Mountain Nature:

Risk, Motive, and Lifestyle in Three Hobbyist Sports

Robert A. Stebbins
University of Calgary

DETSELIG
ENTERPRISES LTD

Challenging Mountain Nature
© 2005 Robert A. Stebbins

Library and Archives Canada Cataloguing in Publication

Stebbins, Robert A., 1938-
    Challenging mountain nature: risk, motive and lifestyle in three
hobbyist sports / Robert A. Stebbins.

Includes bibliographical references and index.
ISBN 1-55059-291-2

1. Kayaking--Psychological aspects. 2. Snowboarding--Psychologi-
cal aspects. 3. Mountaineering--Psychological aspects. 4. Mountains-
Recreational use--Psychological aspects. 5. Risk-taking (Psychology).

GV14.4.S68 2005   796'.01'9   C2005-904463-2

Detselig Enterprises Ltd.   **D**   www.temerondetselig.com
210, 1220 Kensington Road NW   Email: temeron@telusplanet.net
Calgary, Alberta DETSELIG Phone: (403) 283-0900
T2N 3P5 ENTERPRISES LTD Fax: (403) 283-6947

We acknowledge the support of the Government of Canada through
the Book Publishing Industry Development Program (BPIDP) for our
publishing program.

We also acknowledge the support of the Alberta Foundation for the
Arts for our publishing program.

SAN 113-0234   *Snowboarding photo courtesy of Kevin Walkes*
Printed in Canada   *Cover Design by Alvin Choong*

To Lou Holscher
scrambler *extraordinaire*

Table of Contents

Preface 7

Acknowledgements 11

Chapter 1 Mountain Hobbies:High Risk or Nature-Challenge? . 13

Chapter 2 Leisure: Serious, Casual, and Project-Based 29

Chapter 3 Three Hobbies in Historical Perspective 47

Chapter 4 Leisure Careers 67

Chapter 5 Costs, Rewards, and Motivation 89

Chapter 6 Lifestyles and Social Worlds 103

Chapter 7 Finding an Optimal Leisure Lifestyle 119

Appendix: Interview Guide for Kayakers 137

References 141

Index 149

Preface

I fell in love with the Rocky Mountains on the Alberta-British Columbia border shortly after my arrival in Calgary in 1976 to assume a post in the Department of Sociology at the University of Calgary. Their beauty was undeniable, to be sure, but I quickly learned that it was the many outdoor activities they offered that constituted, for me at least, their true magnetism. They seemed to provide something for nearly everyone, from camping, picnicking, fishing, hunting, and horseback riding to hiking, skiing, cycling, kayaking, snowboarding, mountain climbing, and backpacking. The area is, as well, a photographer's paradise, and wild flower enthusiasts have, quite literally, a field day here. I went in for cross-country skiing (mixed with some snowshoeing) and hiking, which shortly evolved into scrambling (Class 2 and 3 mountain climbing).

My steady participation in these two soon acquainted me with the culture of the various "nature-challenge hobbies," a distinctive subcategory of mountain activities centered on surmounting a natural challenge such as descending a roaring river or steep snow slope, climbing a rock face, or negotiating a rugged trail. Many elements comprise this culture, including shared beliefs about the vagaries of the weather, the habits of the wild animals (bears are the most talked about), the peculiarities of the physical environment, the characteristics of the hobbyists themselves, the nature of their equipment, and so on. But most universal of all is the widely shared interest in risk associated with physical danger, which touches each of the aforementioned elements and others not listed here.

Some physically dangerous risk, nature-challenge culture has it, is abhorred, and therefore to be avoided wherever possible. No one wants to suddenly break a ski, meet a grizzly face to face, be swallowed up by an avalanche, get caught in a blizzard, or deal with a host of other possible outdoor woes. But then there is "voluntary risk," as Stephen Lyng puts it; risk that some of these hobbyists deliberately court for the thrill that such action delivers. Lyng is speaking of "high risk," but it is questionable how many mountain hobbyists actually do voluntarily seek such risk and, for the truly high-risk takers, how often they do this and at which level of danger. This matter is explored in Chapter 1.

Talk about physical high risk leads to a broader discussion of a person's motivation to take up one or more nature-challenge hobbies, motivation as found in a search for deep self-fulfillment through experiencing the many personal and social rewards available in this kind of serious leisure (as balanced against costs). High risk, in the rare instances when voluntarily sought, is but one of many motives for pursuing these hobbies. Further, the narrow concern with high risk has blinkered social scientists to the wider range of motivational forces operating in this sphere of leisure. Many of these forces are far more central to the participant's attraction to the activity than is voluntary high risk, if the latter is an attraction at all.

Just as motivating, in fact, are the leisure careers and leisure lifestyles that nature-challenge hobbyists have fashioned for themselves as they pursue their hobbies over the years. Career and lifestyle fall, however, at the mesostructural level of analysis of these hobbies, a way of studying them that has only rarely been followed by social scientists working in this area. "Mesostructure" is David Maines's (1982) term for the level of analysis found between the levels of direct social interaction (microstructure) and abstract formations of community and society (macrostructure). Instead, scholarly attention has only danced around such questions, having been centered almost exclusively on micro phenomena in psychology and social psychology, on the one hand, or on macro phenomena in sociology, on the other, with high risk being the heavily favored subject of analysis.

To shed some empirical light on these seriously understudied mesostructural and motivational concerns, I conducted a qualitative/exploratory interview and participant observational study of kayakers, snowboarders, and mountain and ice climbers, with each group seeking a markedly different challenge in nature (presented by water, snow, and rock/ice, respectively). The study took place due west of Calgary in the Canmore-Banff area of the Rocky Mountains, an area internationally renowned for its plethora of outdoor pursuits venues. Most of the respondents lived in Canmore, and pursued their hobbies on the nearby rivers, snow slopes, rock faces, and frozen water falls. The object of the study was to develop grounded theory about the leisure careers, lifestyles, and motivation of these three groups of hobbyists. These research interests are primarily mesostructural and, when it comes to cost and rewards, social psychological. The theoretical framework of sensitizing concepts used to guide the research, its analysis, and its writing was that of serious and casual leisure.

This study reveals the power of attraction contained in the nature-challenge hobbies. Their appeal deeply affects not only the hobbyist's work and family life but also that person's other leisure activities. And this appeal prevails despite the variety of costs that each group confronts. But these costs notwithstanding, the participants in this study have, for the most part, found their optimal leisure lifestyle in which self-development and self-fulfillment are maximized, a personal goal often attained by reducing desires in other areas of life, frequently that of work. Even then, their quality of life has reached a personal high point.

Acknowledgements

I am deeply grateful to Sherry Kranabitter, who conducted the interviews and participation observation for this study. Her solid intellectual background in leisure studies, extensive familiarity with the Canmore-Banff mountain hobbies scene, and unbridled enthusiasm for this project made her as ideal a research assistant as I could have ever hoped to find. She contributed further with a careful critical reading of the finished manuscript, for which I am likewise grateful. I also wish to thank Leslie-Anne Keown for her most thorough and punctual library search on the literature bearing on high risk in sport. Augustine Brannigan, Erin Gibbs-Van Brunschot, and two anonymous reviewers selected by the publisher critically read the manuscript, and made many helpful suggestions for improving it. Their efforts are deeply appreciated. Finally, I am indebted to Kim-Marie Ward for her editorial acumen and fine sense of book design.

I also wish to acknowledge the generous financial support for this study provided by the Social Sciences and Humanities Research Council of Canada (SSHRC) through its Standard Research Grants Program (File number 410-2000-0616, grant period: 2000-2003). In addition the Faculty of Social Sciences at the University of Calgary supplied a most welcome development grant that greatly facilitated preparation of the SSHRC grant proposal.

The fine work of Kim Ward, the copy-editor assigned to this project, is evident throughout. Deeply appreciated in particular are her critical eye for catching stylistic and logical flaws and her creative sense of design and layout of the pages of this book.

Chapter 1

Mountain Hobbies:
High Risk or Nature-Challenge?

Come live with me, and be my love;
we will all the pleasures prove
that valleys, groves, hills, and fields,
woods or steepy mountain yields.

Christopher Marlowe,
The Passionate Shepherd to his Love [c. 1589]

Much has been written of late in both the popular press and the scientific literature about "extreme sport," so-called physically dangerous, high-risk activity undertaken for, among other reasons, the intense thrills it apparently offers. Such risk, referred to from hereon simply as risk, is "voluntary risk" (Lyng, 1990), as opposed to abhorred risk, felt in, for example, an uncertain surgery, terrorist threat, or an impending hurricane or tornado. Common belief has it that people go in for voluntary, high-risk activities expressly *because* they endanger life and limb of the participant, even at the individual's superior level of competence to execute them. In such sport, risk of this sort is said to be intrinsically valued and, for this reason, searched for, contrasting sharply with the rest of sport, where risk may sometimes be present but where participants go to great lengths to minimize it, if not avoid it altogether.

The "high-risk" sports, which are attracting ever more participants (Pedersen, 1997), include kayaking, snowboarding, "canyoning" (exploring a canyon as by rafting or climbing), mountain climbing, and free-style rock climbing as well as downhill skiing, sport parachuting, and auto and motorcycle racing. It is also true, although much less often commented on in either journalistic or scientific circles, that some of these activities have ordinary counterparts: pursuits held, in the participant's eyes, to involve low risk. Indeed, this second set of pursuits is the more prevalent of the two, even if much less often in the spotlight. Nonetheless, the popularity of these ordinary pursuits borrows from the notoriety of their extreme cousins.

A great deal of social scientific information is already available on a number of specialized topics related to high-risk participation in some of these sports. The literature tends to fall into two distinct areas. First, a sizeable psychological literature exists, centered primarily on high risk itself, particularly on emotion, birth order, motivation, and personality, as these relate to engaging in risky activity (for a summary see, Slanger & Rudestam, 1997; Nixon, 1981). Second, a smaller macrosociological literature has sprung up around such questions as the place of high-risk sport in modern society, youth culture, and the sprawling realm of leisure consumption (e.g., Egner et al, 1998; Griffiths, 1970; Humphreys, 1997; Midol, 1993; Midol & Broyer, 1995). Stephen Lyng's (1990) famous essay on "edgework" stands as a singular attempt to bridge and integrate the two approaches.

But just how physically dangerous are these activities for people who engage in them? The short answer to this question is that, with rare exceptions, they are not at all risky in any significant sense, for were this true, these people would not likely be involved in them. That is, hobbyists in these fields would like to live another day free of injury to pursue their leisure passion and perhaps do some other interesting things in life. Thus it is for the large majority of interviewees in the study reported here and, as these results suggest, others like them, that savoring possible great danger is by no means the most accurate way to describe their powerful attraction to the core activities that make up their so-called high-risk sports. Instead, this finding privileges an alternative conception, one that also opens the door to a rich motivational and mesostructural (see later) analysis of these activities, namely the idea that they are hobbies centered on meeting particular challenges faced in nature.

Note, for this and subsequent chapters, that, in sloughing off the pursuit of high-risk as a common motive in these activities, I am in no way arguing that low and improbable risk are therefore also unimportant. Both are in fact present in the three mountain activities, but nevertheless, participants either manage them, thereby reducing their danger, or ignore them, because danger is unlikely. Further, note that, throughout, discussions of risk center exclusively on the physically-dangerous variety and thus not on other kinds of uncertainty as found, for instance, in the health, economic, and occupational spheres of life.

The Nature-Challenge Hobbies

Nature-challenge, as adjective, is more accurate for describing the three sports covered in this book than any of the more popular alternative adjectives, among them risk, extreme, adventure (as risk), and sensation seeking. Even the locution "mountain sport," the one with which this research project actually began, now seems after having gathered the data, to be inadequate as a descriptor. Why? Because kayaking, snowboarding, and mountaineering (including ice climbing) – the three activities investigated in this study – are certainly not always pursued as sport. But, if the idea of high risk is too problematic as an explanation of dangerous activity, what will work in its place? What is needed is a conceptual framework that describes, or at least helps describe, what deeply interests people in these sports, what powerfully draws them to the core activity and keeps them enthusiastically going back for more? The possibility of getting killed or maimed, when examined carefully, hardly seems like a reasonable answer to this question.

An especially intriguing challenge of nature as met by executing the component tasks comprising a distinctive core, or central, leisure activity filled this requirement for all the participants studied in the three hobbies. The mountaineers have fallen in love with the deep self-fulfillment that comes with meeting the challenge of climbing a rock face or frozen waterfall, the snowboarders with meeting that of descending a steep snow covered slope or doing tricks in the snowboard park, and the kayakers with meeting that of negotiating stretches of white water in a river. True, within each hobby, they sometimes compete with each other for best times (and, in snowboarding sometimes, also for best form) in accomplishing these things, but most often they compete only against what nature offers. This may include certain human modifications such as snowboard park constructions for snowboarders, embedded bolts for mountain climbers, and artificial hazards erected for kayaking races. The natural challenge is, in every instance, the common denominator in all this.

Theoretically speaking, nature-challenge hobbies are not essentially sports, since most of the time, interhuman competition based on a recognized set of rules, an essential element in sport (Coakley, 2001, p. 20), is absent. Be that as it may, I will occasionally refer to these hobbies as sports, simply because this is accepted usage both among the interviewees and in the popular mind. Moreover, some nature-challenge hobbyists do go in for the occasional competition, becoming for the moment hobbyist sports participants in their activities. The characteristics of hobbies, in general, and nature-challenge hobbies, in particular, are more fully considered in the next chapter.

The motives for taking up a nature-challenge hobby (sport) are many and intricately interrelated. Indeed, several sections of this book are devoted exclusively to this matter. I would like to foreshadow some of this discussion by noting here that, while such activity is deeply fulfilling and thus strongly motivating, it is also, when at its height, intensely thrilling. That is, it is fun, exhilarating, and at times, a peak experience. But this is not the language of physically dangerous risk; rather it is the language of leisure and psychological flow (Csikszentmihalyi, 1990). Meeting a particular challenge of nature is captivating, in significant part, because doing so enables the participant to find self-fulfillment in flow and leisure. For instance one kayaker enthused: "the most pleasure I ever get is just surfing the wave, you just turn your mind off. It is like Yoga. I am just trying to dance on a wave; surfing on a wave is the greatest pleasure on earth. So what identifies us as people, inner calm?" ("Standing waves" are mounds or ridges of rushing water.) Time stops, consciousness narrows. Whitewater kayakers think of nothing else than what they are doing at the moment on that river that day.

Being in flow in these activities, as opposed to experiencing leisure in the sports more generally, presupposes *manageable* challenge, however, nothing too easy, which is boring, but nothing too difficult, which in these sports can be terrifying. *Flow*, an idea discussed more fully in the next chapter, is most intense when people operate at or near their mental and physical limits, but stop short of going beyond them. Additionally, whether someone is in flow, depends on that person's amount of experience, level of native talent as well as acquired skill and knowledge in the activity. High loadings on these dimensions raise the mental and physical limits; that is they raise the level of manageability. This gives some nonparticipants who are watching the participant in action the impression that the latter is facing danger and high risk. But the participant is not of this opinion.

This is the essence of why I reject the idea of high physical risk as a general descriptor of these activities. High physical risk in sport has to do with reasonable likelihood of perceived danger at a given level of experience, talent, and so on, that holds out significant probability of major injury, even death. Our interviewees undertake their serious leisure to beat nature in a particular way, sometimes pushing their limits to do so, and from time to time experience flow as a result. Taking great risk, as they define it, abruptly and dramatically diminishes the feeling of flow, for such risk emerges unexpectedly, feeding on the sense that the activity has now become frighteningly unmanageable. With this change in meaning of the activity goes one of the main reasons for doing it in the first place. In vernacular terms, it is no longer fun.

Now, it is true, as Donnelly (2004, p. 44) has observed, that people may, in response to peer pressure, take unacceptable risks (as personally defined) in sports of the kind being considered here. They may also suddenly find themselves in greatly risky situations not of their making, as caused by unexpected changes in weather or conditions of the course (stretch of water, snow slope, mountain face) or unexpected failure of equipment. Faced with such contingencies the individual may be unable to leave, transforming into coerced activity what was previously considered (uncoerced) leisure. This is not, however, why they are so strongly drawn to the activity. Indeed, such experiences could lead some of them to abandon it in the future, as happened to a few of the participants in this study. The "epics" discussed in Chapter 4, during which risk becomes unacceptably high, are cut from this cloth of the unexpected.

Concerning high risk in the area of nature-challenge hobbies, there are, then, as seen through the eyes of the hobbyists, at least four types. *Unmanaged high risk*, or risk that emerges only when individuals lose concentration, get fatigued, or otherwise suddenly become unable to draw on their acquired skills, knowledge, and experience that keep them in leisure and, at its peak, in flow. The second is *fortuitous high risk*, or greatly improbable risk from uncontrollable sources such as snow avalanches, falling rock, sudden elevations of water level (as caused by heavy rain), and ice slicks (on cross-country ski trails). What mountaineers call "objective hazards," hazards created by nature. Consider the following example:

> Two Canmore sisters [not mountaineers] were
> collecting rocks on a family hike in the Rockies
> when a huge gust of wind toppled an 18-metre

spruce tree on top of them, their father told the *Herald* on Tuesday.

The accident happened at about 2:30 p.m. Monday at Marble Canyon, a hiking trail on Highway 93S., about 15 kilometres southwest of Castle Mountain in Kootenay National Park.

Parks staff said winds in the area were extremely high.

Several trees were reported to have blown over on another path in the area and in a nearby campground, said Shelley Humphries, spokeswoman for Parks Canada.

"It's not unusual for trees to fall (in the area)," said Humphries. "What is unusual is that someone was hurt."

With their parents, Peggy and Paul, the sisters were walking across the upper bridges of the canyon when the tree fell on them. (Poole, 2003, p., A1)

Social high risk, the third type, was presented earlier as pressure from peers to engage in the activity at a level regarded by the pressured participant as risky, in other words, it is regarded by that person as going significantly beyond his or her acquired skills, knowledge, and experience. But social risk can also include intentionally taking great risks for the fame, and perhaps, even the fortune that it brings. As example of this latter orientation consider that of Régine Cavagnoud, French world champion in alpine skiing, who died in a collision with a ski coach while hurtling down a slope in the Alps.

Many times previously Miss Cavagnoud had been badly injured on the slopes while pushing herself to her natural limits, and probably beyond, in her drive to become a world champion. . . . Miss Cavagnoud did feel fear. Considering the risks involved, there have been relatively few deaths on the slopes. . . . But many skiers are badly injured. Miss Cavagnoud dreaded ending up in a wheelchair. But even more, she said, she dreaded doing badly (*The Economist,* 2001b).

A number of popular books also celebrate taking intentional social risk in nature, thereby contributing disproportionately to the commonsense notion that the hobbies in question are inherently hazardous (e.g., Jon Krakauer, *Into Thin Air* [1997]; Sabastian Junger, *The Perfect Storm* [1999]; Jonathan Shay *Achilles in Viet Nam* [1995]).

And sometimes nature-challenge hobbyists take social risks because others in their team want to press on (e.g., up the mountain face, down the river rapids). An important point to be made about their activities is that the first two types of risk can, with careful preparation and advance information, usually be avoided and, in fact, generally are. They are avoided because, in significant part, even moderate risk seriously dilutes the senses of flow and leisure. It is questionable whether either is felt at all in social risk, though that may not matter in any case, since the object here is to establish an identity as "gutsy," as a devil-may-care individual. Let us look at this female kayaker's early experiences in her hobby:

> R: I did more than I should have done. Spent a lot of time on the Kananaskis [River], and then paddled sort of on even some class 3 stuff. But a lot of the time I was very discouraged kayaking. I was simply being dragged along by these guys. I'd go on their kayaking trips, and we would go to the Clearwater [River], which scared the hell out me, but everybody was doing it.
>
> I: *Did you just get out and portage on that?*
>
> R: No I swam a lot [bailed out of her kayak]. I portaged a lot too, but mostly I just swam. So the first summer was a lot on the Kan[anaskis] and a few trips elsewhere to bigger rivers, but not that I was necessarily confident on most of them. I was o.k. But I couldn't roll so that was a big thing.

Finally, included in this list is what I call *humanitarian high risk.* For example, Jennifer Lois (2003) studied "peak volunteers" – viewed in the present book according to the serious leisure perspective as leisure participants – who sometimes must challenge nature while carrying out search and rescue missions. They seek high risk not for its own sake, but rather confront it (presumably reluctantly) in their efforts to save lives or recover bodies. Peak volunteers are not hobbyists, of course, so our nature-challenge enthusiasts would encounter such risk only when they also take up this serious leisure role.

In short, while the public, in general, and the press, in particular, are fond of describing mountaineering, kayaking, and snowboarding in dramatic global terms as "high-risk" pursuits, this is not how the vast majority of the interviewees described their routine involvement in them. Even the scientific literature in this field, with some exceptions, has ignored the place of leisure and flow as motivators. Still, Lipscomb (1999) and Celsi, Rose, and Leigh (1993, pp. 11-12) couch their discussions of "high-risk" skydiving squarely in the language of flow, as do Jones, Hollenhorst, and Perna (2003) in their study of kayakers, and Creyer, Ross, and Evers (2003) in their study of mountain bikers. Bratton, Kinnear, and Koroluk (1979) found that "flirting with danger" was the last of 22 reasons their Canadian sample gave for climbing mountains. Lyng's concept of "edgework," or voluntary risk taking, includes the proposition that its skills involve "the ability to maintain control over a situation that verges on complete chaos, a situation that most people would regard as entirely uncontrollable" (Lyng, 1990, p. 859). That ability includes being able to avoid becoming paralyzed by fear, preserving thus one's capacity to focus attention and action on movements critical for survival. Finally, studies of sensation seeking can be conceived of as investigations of selected aspects of the flow experience, even if they tend to neglect the condition of manageable challenge (e.g., Robinson, 1985; Campbell, Tyrrell, & Zingaro, 1993).

Beyond the psychological and macrosociological literature on high risk in sport, including Stephen Lyng's celebrated synthesis, I found a conspicuous absence of intermediate level, or mesostructural, theory and research on these hobbyist sports and activities. "Mesostructure" is David Maines's (1982) term for the level of analysis found between the levels of direct social interaction (microstructure) and abstract formations like community and society (macrostructure). Here we find research on such structures as small groups and social networks, as well as on what Hall (1987) calls "collective activity," or the coordinated sequences of acts carried out by two or more persons in relation to a certain goal (e.g., executing a play in hockey, climbing a rock face with help form other climbers). The concept of the "social world," one of the defining qualities of serious leisure to be introduced in the next chapter, is a mesostructural idea. Finally, the study of leisure lifestyles, whether casual or serious, seems most accurately conceived of as belonging on this level of analysis.

Ethnographically oriented investigations typically contain a number of mesostructural observations, and the present one is no exception. Such theory and research bear on, among other phenomena, the leisure careers and lifestyles of the hobbyists in this study. Thus, from the mesostructural standpoint, interest lies in their involvement in the core activity as well as their preparation for it, the way they relate it to friends and relatives who are not involved, and how they mold their own participation in it around their personal and occupational obligations, and serious and casual leisure interests.

Finally, single-minded concentration on high risk has also led to scientific neglect of many other, far more central, motivational elements that inspire deep and extensive participation in the core hobbyist activities considered here. As shown later in this book the psychology and social psychology explaining pursuit of these mountain hobbies are far more complicated than one dramatic motive – seeking high risk – even in those rare instances when it is a true mainspring for action.

The Study

This study explored along three principal avenues the nature-challenge hobbies of kayaking, mountain climbing, and snowboarding. The first avenue is that of the lifestyle (Stebbins, 1997b) that goes with each of these hobbies. Knowledge of these lifestyles can add greatly to what we have learned about nature-challenge activities in general using macrosociological and psychological perspectives. For one, lifestyle analysis of an activity shows how participants mobilize the resources (e.g., time, money, social support) needed to engage in it. This relates, in part, to certain social class determinants of leisure consumption. Two, such analysis also reveals participants' organizational and social world ties (Unruh, 1979; 1980) and how they facilitate or hinder their participation in the central activity.

Three, lifestyle analysis of a central life interest (Dubin, 1992), as nature-challenge sport is by definition, brings to centre stage the question of identity, both personal and social. For many serious leisure enthusiasts, their leisure becomes a main signpost telling the rest of the world who they are and what they stand for. Four, lifestyle analysis includes examination of other leisure activities and the ways they relate, in the present instance, to the nature-challenge activity. For example, some mountain climbers become ice climbers in the winter, while some cross-country skiers keep fit during the summer by cycling. In other words, I found that, over a typical year, the respondents interviewed tend to engage in several nature-challenge activities, those studied here being but one of those activities. Indeed some hardy souls with ample time even pursued a couple of them during the same season (e.g., snowboarding and downhill skiing). The concepts of social world, lifestyle, and central life interest, forming part of the theory of serious leisure as they do, are treated in greater detail in Chapter 2.

Lifestyle analysis tends to be static, however, in the sense that it consists of analysis of everyday life at a particular time in the history of the hobby and the life cycle of the people under study. This calls for the second line of research: the life cycle perspective, expressed here in a focus on career. Examination of leisure careers (Stebbins, 1992) of participants in nature-challenge hobbies helps overcome this deficiency, centering as it does on how participants get interested in the sport, develop it to their present level of competence, and plan for its future continuation, all in the context of changing interpersonal and occupational forces (family responsibilities, occupational career contingencies, injury through participation in the activity, etc.). Moreover, just as leisure activity varies over a participant's life cycle, the sport itself has a history, as founded on collective definitions of attraction, competence, and aesthetics as well as advances in equipment. For this reason, a history of each hobby as a collective or cultural form is presented in Chapter 3, culminating in a set of observations about its place in contemporary society.

By way of illustration, "conquests" such as ascending Mount Everest are recognized as forms of cultural capital that translate into personal prestige, however nonutilitarian the accomplishment. And, in harmony with this principle, I observed within each of the three nature-challenge sports an informal, local stratification system based on benchmark achievements, which gives substance to Bourdieu's concept of "distinction" (1979), an idea only tangentially related to social class.

This system clearly differentiates the "devotee" enthusiast from the more ordinary "participant." Hobbyists highly dedicated to their pursuits have been referred to as devotees (Stebbins, 1992, p. 46). When they are only moderately interested, but significantly more so than dabblers, they are called participants. Participants typically greatly outnumber devotees. Along this dimension devotees and participants are operationally distinguished primarily by the different amounts of time they commit to their hobby, as manifested in engaging in the core activity, training for it, reading about it, and the like.

No study of nature-challenge hobbyist activity would be complete without a third component, namely, exploration of the costs and rewards of such activity. In this regard I tackled directly the question of motivation for pursuing such interests, their flow properties, their costs, and the principles these hobbyists use to offset the latter. Here is where the putative risky nature of these hobbies is found to be inadequate, both in terms of what they mean for the participants and, by extension, as valid explanation of them for scientific purposes. The study of motivation in this book is basically social psychological, but with many mesostructural overtones, most notably the social rewards.

To learn more about the careers and lifestyles of nature-challenge hobbyists, I studied these two broad mesostructural segments of everyday life as experienced by kayakers, snow-boarders, and mountain and ice climbers. These three activities are pursued in the Canadian Rockies on three different kinds of surface (water, snow, rock/ice), and in each, low, moderate, and high-challenge involvement are clearly demarcated using formal classification systems (these are described in Chapter 3). As with many of the other nature-challenge hobbies, substantial macrosociological and psychological literature (e.g., Pociello, 1991; Campbell, Tyrrell, & Zingaro, 1993, Ewert & Hollenhorst, 1994) exists on all three, whereas the mesostructural level has virtually escaped scientific attention. Indeed, I could find only two exceptions to this observation, both on mountain climbing (Mitchell, 1983; Williams & Donnelly, 1985).

Why study kayaking, snowboarding, and mountain climbing instead of three other mountain sports? In part, the decision to study these three was based on convenience: they exist in the mountains near Calgary where I live and are pursued by large numbers of enthusiasts. And they do represent activities that challenge the three natural elements of water, snow, and rock/ice. True, mountain biking, alpine foot racing, and downhill skiing, three other nature-challenge activities carried out on snow and rock, could have been examined in lieu of climbing and boarding, but this is an exploratory study not a survey. A sample of the sports using the three natural elements is all that is called for at this point in the development of the mesostructural analysis of natural challenge hobbies. Interestingly, the fourth natural element – air – is seldom challenged in the mountains, for parachuting and hang gliding in this environment, for example, are generally considered too risky.

To facilitate comparison, I included low- medium- and high-challenge participants in the study, with the range of level of challenge being sampled approximately equally. Twenty-three climbers (ice and mountain), 16 snowboarders, and 24 kayakers were interviewed (N=63), samples that included the vast majority of all possible interviewees available at the time of data collection. Table 1 contains the age and sex distributions of the three samples. Demographic data on occupation, education, and marital status are presented in Chapter 6 in conjunction with the analysis of lifestyle and social world. The study also included extensive participant observation of participants at all three levels of challenge in action as kayakers, snowboarders, and ice and mountain climbers (to the extent possible and safe for the researcher) and related activities such as club

Table 1				
Age and Sex Distribution of Respondents by Sample				
Sample	Average age	Male	Female	Total respondents
Climbers	32.1	13	10	23
Kayakers	32.6	14	10	24
Snowboarders	24.0	8	8	16
Total respondents		35	28	63

meetings, after-hours discussions of outings, and life at equipment suppliers and repair facilities.

The data were collected between May 2000 and April 2002. The interviews were, for the most part, conducted following the sessions of observation. All three samples included both organized and unorganized participants, the latter being recruited for interviewing through the practice of snowball sampling. Observations were made in the Rocky Mountain area west of Calgary, and the interviewees resided in the Calgary-Canmore-Banff corridor, with most living just outside Banff National Park in the town of Canmore where they have the most convenient access possible to the local sites where they pursue their hobbies. (Living in Banff, which in many ways is even more centrally located, is prohibited, unless employed in the National Park.) The corridor in question was scoured in prehistoric times by the Bow River, and is, today, a major rail and highway thoroughfare leading to and from the Pacific Coast. The Canmore-Banff area is world famous for its exceptional opportunities for pursuing a variety of mountain hobbies, and several respondents had, for this reason, moved there from other parts of Canada and from other countries, most notably Australia, New Zealand, and the United Kingdom.

The interviews were usually long, often lasting more than two hours, not an uncommon occurrence in studies of serious leisure where passion and enthusiasm are high for the activity in question. They were conducted by a female doctoral student in sociology, herself a mountaineer, with some experience as well in snowboarding, among several other mountain hobbies. Furthermore, she was well versed in the serious leisure-casual leisure framework. Before she began work on this project, she had lived in Canmore and participated for approximately two years in many facets of its mountain hobby culture.

Since this was a qualitative-exploratory research project, all observations and interviews were conducted in open-ended fashion, with the intention of thereby producing data leading to a grounded theory of the motivational patterns, leisure careers, and personal lifestyles of the three types of hobbyists (Glaser & Strauss, 1967; Glaser, 1978; Stebbins, 2001b). The Appendix contains a copy of the final version of the interview guide used with the kayaking sample. It shows in detail the kinds of data that were collected with reference to these three foci. Exploration of these hobbies generated a variety of new concepts and propositions, a process that was framed by the serious leisure perspective and its many propositions and sensitizing concepts (Stebbins, 1992; 1996; 2001b). Of all the social scientific perspectives, this one is most directly related to the present study and most useful for framing it conceptually and setting initial, albeit flexible, guidelines for inquiry. Serious, casual, and project-based leisure are discussed in the next chapter.

This book, then, is about the motives, leisure careers, and general lifestyles of participants in three nature-challenge hobbies that, in their eyes, are not routinely risky and not sought for their high-risk potential. Nevertheless, they could become significantly more risky should concentration lapse or critical, unexpected, objective hazards suddenly emerge. These hobbies, among many others, are classified as a type of serious leisure pursuit. This study of them adds to the meager literature on hobbies, the least studied of the three forms of serious leisure. Furthermore, it joins an earlier study of barbershop singers (Stebbins, 1996a), becoming one of only two studies of the activity participation type of hobby.

But just what is serious leisure, the leisure of amateurs, hobbyists, and career volunteers?

Chapter 2

Leisure:
Serious, Casual, and Project-Based

> No man is really happy or safe without a hobby,
> and it makes precious little difference what the
> outside interest may be – botany, beetles or butter-
> flies, roses, tulips or irises; fishing, mountaineering
> or antiquities – anything will do so long as he
> straddles a hobby and rides it hard.
>
> Sir William Osler
> *Farewell Dinner* [2 May 1905]

Serious leisure is the systematic pursuit of an amateur, hobbyist, or volunteer activity sufficiently substantial and interesting in nature for the participant to find a career there acquiring and expressing a combination of its special skills, knowledge, and experience (Stebbins, 1992, p. 3). It is typically contrasted with "casual" or "unserious" leisure, which is considerably less substantial and offers no career of the sort just described. It is defined as immediately, intrinsically rewarding, relatively short-lived pleasurable activity, requiring little or no special training to enjoy it (Stebbins, 1997a, p. 18). Although casual leisure was once defined residually as all leisure falling outside the three main types of serious leisure, a third kind of leisure has been observed in recent years. It is project-based leisure: a short-term, reasonably complicated, one-shot or occasional, though infrequent, creative undertaking carried out in free time, or time free of disagreeable obligation (Stebbins, 2005; on obligation and free time, see Stebbins, 2000b). Since the interviewees of this study also engaged in casual and project leisure as part of their overall leisure lifestyle, more will be said about both later in this chapter.

Serious Leisure

Serious leisure is constituted of three types: amateurism, hobbyist activities, and career volunteering. Amateurs are found in art, science, sport, and entertainment, where they are inevitably linked, one way or another, with professional counterparts who coalesce, along with the public whom the two groups share, into a three-way system of relations and relationships (the P-A-P system). The professionals are identified and defined according to theory developed in the social scientific study of the professions, a substantially more exact procedure than the ones relying on the simplistic and not infrequently commercially-shaped commonsense images of these workers. In other words, when studying amateurs and professionals, descriptive definitions turn out to be too superficial, such as observing that the activity in question constitutes a livelihood for the second but not the first or that the second works full-time at it whereas the first pursues it part-time. Rather, we learn much more by noting that, for example, the two are locked in and therefore defined, in most instances, by the P-A-P system, an arrangement too complex to describe further in this book (see Stebbins, 1979; 1992, pp. 38-41; 2002b, pp 129-130).

Hobbyists lack the professional alter ego of amateurs, although they sometimes have commercial equivalents and often have small publics who take an interest in what they do. Hobbyists are classified according to five categories: collectors, makers and tinkerers, activity participants (in noncompetitive, rule-based, pursuits such as fishing and barbershop singing), players of sports and games (in competitive, rule-based activities with no professional counterparts like long-distance running and competitive swimming) and the enthusiasts of the liberal arts hobbies. The rules guiding rule-based pursuits are, for the most part, either subcultural (informal) or regulatory (formal). Thus seasoned hikers in the Rocky Mountains know they should, for example, stay on established trails, pack out all garbage, be prepared for changes in weather, and make noise to scare off bears. The liberal arts hobbyists are enamored of the systematic acquisition of knowledge for its own sake. Many of them accomplish this by reading voraciously in a field of art, sport, cuisine, language, culture, history, science, philosophy, politics, or literature (Stebbins, 1994). But some of them go beyond this to expand their knowledge still further through cultural travel.

The nature-challenge activities fall under the heading of noncompetitive, rule-based activity participation. True, actual competitions are sometimes held in these hobbies (e.g., fastest time over a particular course), but mostly beating nature is thrill enough. Moreover, other nature hobbies exist, which are also challenging, but in very different ways. Some, most notably fishing and hunting, in essence exploit the natural environment. Others center on appreciation of the outdoors, among them hiking, backpacking, bird watching, and horseback riding (Stebbins, 1998b, p. 59).

Turning next to volunteering, Cnaan, Handy, and Wadsworth (1996) identified four dimensions they found running throughout the several definitions of volunteering they examined. These dimensions are free choice, remuneration, structure, and intended beneficiaries. The following definition has been created from these four: **volunteering** *is uncoerced help offered either formally or informally with no or, at most, token pay and done for the benefit of both other people and the volunteer* (Stebbins, 2004a).

Concerning the free choice dimension, the language of (lack of) "coercion," is preferred since that of "free choice" is hedged about with numerous problems (see Stebbins, 2002a). The logical difficulties of including obligation in definitions of volunteering militate against including this condition in the foregoing definition (see Stebbins, 2001d). As for remuneration, volunteers retain their voluntary spirit providing they avoid becoming dependent on any money received from their volunteering. Structurally, volunteers may serve formally in collaboration with legally chartered organizations or informally in situations involving small groups, sets, or networks of relatives, friends, neighbors, and the like that have no such legal basis. Finally, it follows from what was said previously about altruism and self-interest in volunteering that both the volunteers and those they help find benefits in such activity. It should be noted, however, that the field of serious leisure, or career, volunteering, even if it does cover considerable ground, is still narrower than that of volunteering in general, which includes helping as casual leisure.

The taxonomy published by the author (Stebbins, 1998b, pp. 74-80), which consists of 16 types of organizational volunteering, shows the scope of career volunteering. Career volunteers provide a great variety of services in education, science, civic affairs (advocacy projects, professional and labor organizations), spiritual development, health, economic development, religion, politics, government (programs and services), human relationships, recreation, and the arts. Some of these volunteers work in the fields of safety or the physical environment, while others prefer to provide necessities (e.g., food, clothing, shelter) or support services. Although much of career volunteering appears to be connected in some way with an organization of some sort, the scope of this leisure is possibly even broader, perhaps including the kinds of helping devoted individuals do for social movements or for neighbors and family. Still, the definition of serious leisure restricts attention everywhere to volunteering in which the participant can find a career, in which there is more or less continuous and substantial helping. Therefore, one-time donations of money, organs, services, and the like are more accurately classified as voluntary action of another sort, as are instances of casual volunteering, which include ushering, stuffing envelopes, and handing out programs as an aid to commercial, professional, or serious leisure undertakings (Stebbins, 1996b).

Serious leisure is further defined by six distinguishing qualities (Stebbins, 1992, pp. 6-8), qualities found among amateurs, hobbyists, and volunteers alike. One is the occasional need to *persevere*, such as in confronting danger (Fine, 1988, p. 181), supporting team in losing season (Gibson, Willming, & Holdnak, 2002, pp. 405-408), or embarrassment (Floro, 1978, p. 198). Yet, it is clear that positive feelings about the activity come, to some extent, from sticking with it through thick and thin, from conquering adversity. A second quality is, as already indicated, that of finding a leisure career in the endeavor, shaped as it is by its own special contingencies, turning points and stages of achievement or involvement. Because of the widespread tendency to see the idea of career as applying only to occupations, note that, in this definition, the term is much more broadly used, following Goffman's (1961, pp. 127-128) elaboration of the concept of "moral career." Broadly conceived of, careers are available in all substantial, complicated roles, including especially those in work, leisure, deviance, politics, religion, and interpersonal relationships.

Careers in serious leisure commonly rest on a third quality: significant personal *effort* based on specially acquired *knowledge*, *training*, or *skill*, and, indeed, all three at times. Examples include such characteristics as showmanship, athletic prowess, scientific knowledge, and long experience in a role. Fourth, eight *durable benefits*, or broad outcomes, of serious leisure have so far been identified, mostly from research on amateurs. They are self-actualization, self-enrichment, self-expression, regeneration or renewal of self, feelings of accomplishment, enhancement of self-image, social interaction and belongingness, and lasting physical products of the activity (e.g., a painting, scientific paper, piece of furniture). A further benefit – self-gratification, or the combination of superficial enjoyment and deep satisfaction – is also one of the main benefits of casual leisure, to the extent that the enjoyment part dominates.

A fifth quality of serious leisure is the *unique ethos* that grows up around each instance of it, a central component of which is a special social world where participants can pursue their free-time interests. Unruh (1980, p. 277) developed the following definition:

> A *social world* must be seen as a unit of social organization which is diffuse and amorphous in character. Generally larger than groups or organizations, social worlds are not necessarily defined by formal boundaries, membership lists, or spatial territory. . . . A social world must be seen as an internally recognizable constellation of actors, organizations, events, and practices which have coalesced into a perceived sphere of interest and involvement for participants. Characteristically, a social world lacks a powerful centralized authority structure and is delimited by . . . effective communication and not territory nor formal group membership.

In another paper Unruh added that the typical social world is characterized by voluntary identification, by a freedom to enter into and depart from it (Unruh, 1979). Moreover, because it is so diffuse, ordinary members are only partly involved in the full range of its activities. After all, a social world may be local, regional, multiregional, national, even, international.

Third, people in complex societies such as Canada and the United States are often members of several social worlds. Finally, social worlds are held together, to an important degree, by semiformal, or mediated, communication. They are rarely heavily bureaucratized yet, due to their diffuseness, they are rarely characterized by intense face-to-face interaction. Rather, communication is typically mediated by newsletters, posted notices, telephone messages, mass mailings, Internet communications, radio and television announcements, and similar means, with the strong possibility that the Internet could become the most popular of these in the future.

The sixth quality revolves around the preceding five: participants in serious leisure tend to *identify* strongly with their chosen pursuits. In contrast, casual leisure, though hardly humiliating or despicable, is nonetheless too fleeting, mundane, and commonplace for most people to find a distinctive identity there. In fact, as this study shows, a serious leisure pursuit can hold greater appeal as an identifier than the person's work role.

In addition, research on serious leisure has led to the discovery of a distinctive set of rewards for each activity examined (Stebbins, 2001a, p. 13). In these studies the participant's leisure satisfaction has been found to stem from a constellation of particular rewards gained from the activity, be it boxing, ice climbing, or giving dance lessons to the elderly. Furthermore, the rewards are not only satisfying in themselves, but also satisfying as counterweights to the costs encountered in the activity. That is, every serious leisure activity contains its own combination of tensions, dislikes and disappointments, which each participant must confront in some way. For instance, an amateur football player may not always like attending daily practices, being bested occasionally by more junior players when there, and being required to sit on the sidelines from time to time while others get experience at his position. Yet he may still regard this activity as highly satisfying – as (serious) leisure – because it also offers certain powerful rewards.

Put more precisely, then, the drive to find fulfillment in serious leisure is the drive to experience the rewards of a given leisure activity, such that its costs are seen by the participant as more or less insignificant by comparison. This is at once the meaning of the activity for the participant and his or her motivation for engaging in it. It is this motivational sense of the concept of reward that distinguishes it from the idea of durable benefit set out earlier, an idea that emphasizes outcomes rather than antecedent conditions. Nonetheless, the two ideas constitute two sides of the same social psychological coin.

The rewards of a serious leisure pursuit are the more or less routine values that attract and hold its enthusiasts. Every serious leisure career both frames and is framed by the continuous search for these rewards, a search that takes months, and in many sports, years before the participant consistently finds deep satisfaction in his or her amateur, hobbyist, or volunteer role. The ten rewards presented below emerged in the course of various exploratory studies of amateurs, hobbyists, and career volunteers (for summary of these studies, see Stebbins, 2001a). As the following list shows, the rewards of serious leisure are predominantly personal.

Personal rewards

1. Personal enrichment (cherished experiences)
2. Self-actualization (developing skills, abilities, knowledge)
3. Self-expression (expressing skills, abilities, knowledge already developed)
4. Self-image (known to others as a particular kind of serious leisure participant)
5. Self-gratification (combination of superficial enjoyment and deep satisfaction)
6. Re-creation (regeneration) of oneself through serious leisure after a day's work
7. Financial return (from a serious leisure activity)

Social rewards

8. Social attraction (associating with other serious leisure participants, with clients as a volunteer, participating in the social world of the activity)
9. Group accomplishment (group effort in accomplishing a serious leisure project; senses of helping, being needed, being altruistic)
10. Contribution to the maintenance and development of the group (including senses of helping, being needed, being altruistic in making the contribution)

In the various studies on amateurs, hobbyists, and volunteers, these rewards, depending on the activity, were often given different weightings by the interviewees to reflect their importance relative to each other. Nonetheless, some common ground exists, for the studies on sport, for example, do show that, in terms of their personal importance, most serious leisure participants rank self-enrichment and self-gratification as number one and number two. Moreover, to find either reward, participants must have acquired sufficient levels of relevant skill, knowledge, and experience (Stebbins, 1979; 1993). In other words, self-actualization, which was often ranked third in importance, is also highly rewarding in serious leisure.

Finally, I have argued over the years that amateurs and sometimes even the activities they pursue are marginal in society, for amateurs are neither dabblers nor professionals (see also Stebbins, 1979). Moreover, studies of hobbyists and career volunteers show that they and some of their activities are just as marginal and for many of the same reasons (Stebbins, 1996a; 1998a). Several properties of serious leisure give substance to these observations. One, although seemingly illogical according to common sense, is that serious leisure is characterized empirically by an important degree of positive commitment to a pursuit (Stebbins, 1992, pp. 51-52). This commitment is measured, among other ways, by the sizeable investments of time and energy in the leisure made by its devotees and participants (to be considered further in Chapter 6). Two, serious leisure is pursued with noticeable intentness, with such passion that Erving Goffman (1963, pp. 144-145) once qualified amateurs and hobbyists as the "quietly disaffiliated." People with such orientations toward their leisure are marginal compared with people who go in for the ever-popular forms of casual leisure.

Casual Leisure

Since we have already defined casual leisure, let us look next at its types. They include play (including dabbling), relaxation (e.g., sitting, napping, strolling), passive entertainment (e.g., TV, books, recorded music), active entertainment (e.g., games of chance, party games), sociable conversation, sensory stimulation (e.g., sex, eating, drinking, sight seeing), and casual volunteering (described earlier). It is considerably less substantial and offers no career of the sort described elsewhere for its counterpart, serious leisure (Stebbins, 1992).

This brief review of the types of casual leisure reveals that they share at least one central property: all are hedonic. More precisely, all produce a significant level of pure pleasure, or enjoyment, for those participating in them. In broad, colloquial language, casual leisure could serve as the scientific term for the practice of doing what comes naturally. Yet, paradoxically, this leisure is by no means wholly frivolous, for there are some clear benefits in pursuing it. Moreover, unlike the evanescent hedonic property of casual leisure itself, its benefits are enduring, a property that makes them worthy of extended analysis in their own right.

Benefits

I have so far been able to identify five benefits, or outcomes, of casual leisure. But since this is a preliminary list – my first attempt at making one – it is certainly possible that future research and theorizing could add to it (Stebbins, 2001c).

One lasting benefit of casual leisure is the creativity and discovery it sometimes engenders. Serendipity, "the quintessential form of informal experimentation, accidental discovery, and spontaneous invention" (Stebbins, 2001b), usually underlies these two processes, suggesting that serendipity and casual leisure are at times closely aligned. In casual leisure, as elsewhere, serendipity can lead to highly varied results, including a new understanding of a home gadget or government policy, a sudden realization that a particular plant or bird exists in the neighborhood, or a different way of making artistic sounds on a musical instrument. Such creativity or discovery is unintended, however, and is therefore accidental. Moreover, it is not ordinarily the result of a problem-solving orientation of people taking part in casual leisure, since most of the time at least, they have little interest in trying to solve problems while engaging in such activity. Usually problems for which solutions must be found emerge at work or at home or during serious leisure.

Another benefit springs from what has recently come to be known as *edutainment*. Nahrstedt (2000) holds that this benefit of casual leisure comes with participating in such mass entertainment as watching films and television programs, listening to popular music, and reading popular books and articles. Theme parks and museums are also considered sources of edutainment. While consuming media or frequenting places of this sort, these participants inadvertently learn something of substance about the social and physical world in which they live. They are, in a word, entertained and educated in the same breath.

Third, casual leisure affords regeneration, or re-creation, possibly even more so than its counterpart, serious leisure, since the latter can sometimes be intense. Of course, many a leisure studies specialist has observed that leisure in general affords relaxation or entertainment, if not both, and that these constitute two of its principal benefits. What is new, then, in the observation just made is that it distinguishes between casual and serious leisure, and more importantly, that it emphasizes the enduring effects of relaxation and entertainment when they help enhance overall equanimity, most notably in the interstices between periods of intense activity. Still, strange as it may seem, this blanket recognition of the importance of relaxation has not, according to Kleiber (2000), led to significant concern with it in research and practice in leisure studies.

A fourth benefit that can flow from participation in casual leisure originates in the development and maintenance of interpersonal relationships. One of its types, the sociable conversation, is particularly fecund in this regard, but other types, when shared, as sometimes happens during sensory stimulation, and passive and active entertainment, can also have the same effect. The interpersonal relationships in question are many and varied and encompass those that form between friends, spouses, and members of families.

Well-being is still another benefit that can flow from engaging in casual leisure. Speaking only for the realm of leisure, the greatest sense of well-being is achieved when a person develops an *optimal leisure lifestyle*. Such a lifestyle is,

> the deeply satisfying pursuit during free time of one or more substantial, absorbing forms of serious leisure, complemented by a judicious amount of casual leisure. (Stebbins, 2000)

People find optimal leisure lifestyles by partaking of leisure activities that individually and in combination realize human potential and enhance quality of life and well-being. Project leisure can also enhance a person's leisure lifestyle.

Psychological Flow

Although the idea of flow originated with the work of Mihalyi Csikszentmihalyi 1990) and has therefore an intellectual history quite separate from that of the serious and casual leisure perspective, it does nevertheless happen on occasion that it is a key motivational force in both. In particular, flow is highly prized in the three types of hobbies examined in this book. What then is flow?

The intensity with which some participants approach their leisure suggests that they may at times be in psychological flow there. Flow, a form of optimal experience, is possibly the most widely discussed and studied generic intrinsic reward in the psychology of work and leisure. Although many types of work and leisure generate little or no flow for their participants, those that do are found primarily the "devotee occupations" (Stebbins, 2004b) and serious leisure. Still, it will be evident that each work and leisure activity capable of producing flow does so in terms unique to it. And it follows that each of these activities must be carefully studied to discover the properties contributing to its distinctive flow experience.

In his theory of optimal experience, Csikszentmihalyi (1990, pp. 3-5, 54) describes and explains the psychological foundation of the many flow activities in work and leisure, as exemplified in chess, dancing, surgery, and rock climbing. Flow is "autotelic" experience, or the sensation that comes with the actual enacting of intrinsically rewarding activity. Over the years Csikszentmihalyi (1990, pp. 49-67) has identified and explored eight components of this experience. It is easy to see how this quality of work, when present, is sufficiently rewarding and, it follows, highly valued to endow it with many of the qualities of serious leisure, thereby rendering the two inseparable in several ways. And this even though most people tend to think of work and leisure as vastly different. The eight components are

1. sense of competence in executing the activity;

2. requirement of concentration;

3. clarity of goals of the activity;

4. immediate feedback from the activity;

5. sense of deep, focused involvement in the activity;

6. sense of control in completing the activity;

7. loss of self-consciousness during the activity;

8. sense of time is truncated during the activity.

These components are self-evident, except possibly for the first and the sixth. With reference to the first, flow fails to develop when the activity is either too easy or too difficult; to experience flow the participant must feel capable of performing a moderately challenging activity. The sixth component refers to the perceived degree of control the participant has over execution of the activity. This is not a matter of personal competence;

rather it is one of degree of influence of uncontrollable external forces, a condition well illustrated in situations faced by the hobbyists in this study, such as when the water level suddenly rises on the river or an unpredicted snowstorm results in a whiteout on a mountain snowboard slope.

Flow is a cardinal motivator in mountaineering, kayaking, and snowboarding, even while it is only an occasional state of mind. That is, in any given outing in one of these hobbies, participants only experience flow some of the time. Meanwhile it is not even this central, or even present at all, in some other outdoor hobbies. It does not, for instance, seem to characterize much of mountain scrambling, backpacking, or horseback riding. By contrast, it is certainly a motivational feature in mountain biking and cross-country and downhill skiing.

Project-Based Leisure

Project-base leisure (Stebbins, 2005) requires considerable planning, effort, and sometimes skill or knowledge, but is for all that neither serious leisure nor intended to develop into such. Examples include surprise birthday parties, elaborate preparations for a major holiday, and volunteering for sports events. Though only a rudimentary social world springs up around the project, it does in its own particular way bring together friends, neighbors, or relatives (e.g., through a genealogical project or Christmas celebrations), or draw the individual participant into an organizational milieu (e.g., through volunteering for a sports event or major convention).

This further suggests that project-based leisure often has, in at least two ways, potential for building community. One, it can bring into contact people who otherwise have no reason to meet, or at least meet frequently. Two, by way of event volunteering and other collective altruistic activity, it can contribute to carrying off community events and projects. Project-based leisure is not, however, civil labor (i.e., long-term, uncoerced work without pay that contributes to community development), which must be classified, as Rojek (2002) has recently argued, as exclusively serious leisure. The mountain hobbyists in the present study occasionally rounded out their leisure lifestyles by undertaking or participating in projects of this kind.

Leisure Lifestyle

Lifestyle is

> a distinctive set of shared patterns of tangible behavior that is organized around a set of coherent interests or social conditions or both. It is explained and justified by a set of related values, attitudes, and orientations and, under certain conditions, becomes the basis for a separate, common social identity for its participants. (Stebbins, 1997b, p. 350)

A profound lifestyle awaits anyone who routinely pursues a serious leisure career in, say, amateur theater, volunteer work with the mentally handicapped, the hobby of model railroading, or that of mountain kayaking or snowboarding. And it is possible that this person also finds exciting, albeit clearly less profound, lifestyles in such casual leisure pastimes as socializing in hot tubs and "whooping it up" at weekend beer parties. But many other forms of casual leisure, for example routine people watching and strolling in the park, are usually not shared with large numbers of other people and therefore cannot be considered lifestyles according to the preceding definition. Moreover, in themselves, these activities are too superficial and unremarkable to serve as the basis for a recognizable mode of living.

This study marks the first attempt, as far as I know, to examine in a sample of leisure participants not only their serious leisure but also their casual and project-based leisure. The results are presented in Chapter 7, where I discuss optimal leisure lifestyle and its composition among these hobbyists. It turns out that optimal leisure lifestyle cannot be considered in isolation, as a solitary free time phenomenon, for there must be enough time and availability of desirable leisure for such a lifestyle to emerge. A heavy schedule of work and nonwork obligations can easily scotch any possibility of achieving an optimal leisure lifestyle.

Optimal Leisure Lifestyle

The foregoing discussion of the three forms of leisure as they relate to leisure lifestyle brings us to the question of how to optimize the latter. Earlier I defined optimal leisure lifestyle, and observed that a person finds one by engaging in leisure activities that individually and in combination realize human potential and enhance quality of life and personal well-being. People seeking to optimize their leisure this way strive to get the best return they can from use of free time. What is considered "best" is, of course, a matter of personal definition; quality of optimal leisure lifestyle is predicated on a person's awareness of much of the great range of potentially available leisure possibilities. Thus people know they have reached it when, from their own reasonably wide knowledge of feasible serious and casual leisure activities and associated costs and rewards, they can say they have enhanced their free-time well-being to the fullest by having found the best combination of the two types, perhaps punctuated from time to time with some project-based leisure.

A highly satisfying life of leisure is predicated, in part, on a workable schedule of all leisure activities as well as involvement, where possible and desirable, in formal and informal organizations (e.g., chartered associations, small groups of friends) that have, in their own right, substantial leisure appeal (Stebbins, 2002b). Optimally, then, organized involvements will be temporally and geographically spaced such that participants avoid feeling pressed to get to one from another. Moreover, organized activities will be complementary. Thus, it is hardly optimal to have scheduled an enervating afternoon session of whitewater kayaking before an evening rehearsal of the local barbershop chorus, which will entail at least two hours of standing on risers accompanied by plenty of diaphragm work. Finally, note that an optimal leisure lifestyle can only be a goal for people pursuing more than one leisure activity, which they do in the course of the customary divisions of time: week, month, season, and year.

Identity and Central Life Interest

To the extent that lifestyles form around complicated, absorbing, fulfilling activities, as they invariably do in serious leisure, they can also be viewed as behavioral expressions of participants' "central life interests" in those activities. In his book by the same title, Robert Dubin (1992, p. 41) defines this interest as "that portion of a person's total life in which energies are invested in both physical/intellectual activities and in positive emotional states." Sociologically, a central life interest is often associated with a major role in life. Since they can only emerge from positive emotional states, obsessive and compulsive activities, Dubin says, can never become central life interests.

Dubin's (1992, pp. 41-42) examples clearly establish that either work or serious leisure can become a central life interest:

> A workaholic is an individual who literally lives and breathes an occupation or profession. Work hours know no limits, and off-work hours are usually filled with work-related concerns. Nothing pleases a workaholic more than to be working. Such an individual has a CLI [central life interest] in work.

> A dedicated amateur or professional athlete will devote much more time and concentration to training than will be invested in actual competition. Over and over again athletes will practice their skills, hoping to bring themselves to a peak of performance. Even though practicing may be painful, the ultimate competitive edge produced by practice far outweighs in satisfaction and pride any aches and pains of preparation. Such people make their athletic life their CLI.

> A committed gardener, stamp collector, opera buff, jet setter, cook, housewife, mountain climber, bird watcher, computer "hacker," novel reader,

fisherman, or gambler (and you can add many more to the list from your own experiences) are all usually devoted to their activity as a central life interest. Give such individuals a chance to talk freely about themselves and they will quickly reveal their CLI through fixation on the subject and obvious emotional fervor with which they talk about it.

These are hobbyist and amateur activities. But career volunteers find a lively central life interest in their pursuits, too:

In American politics, and probably the politics of most Western countries, groups increasingly enter political life with a single issue as their rallying point. That single issue may be taxes, abortion, women's rights, the environment, consumerism, conservatism, or civil rights, and much activity and emotion is invested in "the movement." Adherents come to view themselves as personifying "good guys" who rally around a movement's single issue, making their movement their CLI.

As happens with leisure lifestyle, a leisure identity also arises in parallel with a person's leisure-based central life interest. In other words, that person's lifestyle in a given serious leisure activity gives expression to his or her central life interest there, while forming the basis for a personal and community identity as someone who goes in for and is reasonably adept at that activity.

Conclusions

The serious/casual/project-based leisure perspective provided a generalized theoretical framework of sensitizing concepts for exploratory data collection in this study. In later chapters it will be used to organize the reporting of those data on the motivation, leisure careers, and lifestyles of the sampled kayakers, snowboarders, and climbers of rock and ice. Before that, however, it is necessary to place the three mountain hobbies in proper historical context, thereby giving the study some needed chronologic depth.

Chapter 3

Three Hobbies in Historical Perspective

Great things are done when men and mountains meet;
This is not done by jostling in the street.

William Blake
Epigrams [1808-1811]

Kayaking, snowboarding, and mountain climbing have highly different origins and, as leisure activities, each has a very different longevity. Still, all three have in common that they have benefited from key technological advances which have dramatically changed the course of their histories. Then there is the matter of popularity. In competition with other flow-generating activities in the field of outdoor pursuits, these three have maintained their share of market appeal with particular segments of the population (*The Economist*, 1999; *The Economist*, 1998).

The histories of the three hobbies, along with descriptions of each as a leisure activity, are presented in this chapter in order of their longevity as recognized free-time pursuits: mountain climbing, kayaking, and snowboarding. The histories are short, intended only to provide background for the central focus of the study: the present-day mesostructure of the three. Note, further, that these histories, especially those of kayaking and snowboarding, tend to stress the competitive side of the activity, whereas the hobbyists in this study go in mainly for its non-competitive side. The historical literature in these fields seems, in general, to underplay, if not overlook, the appeal of the pure natural challenge inherent in them. Finally, the histories recount the global evolution of, and involvement in, each hobby rather than its evolution and involvement in the Canadian Rockies, the aim here being to provide background for further research on mesostructure carried out in other parts of the world.

Mountain Climbing

Mountain Climbing, in its broadest sense, is simply ascending on foot, to the summit of a mountain or hill high enough to be a challenge. Whereas people have always climbed these natural protrusions and for all sorts of reasons (e.g., religious experience, military surveillance, scientific research), they have probably always ascended them primarily in the name of leisure. The motives and rewards for such leisure are examined later, and are far more complicated and profound than implied in George Mallory's flippant remark that he wanted to climb Mount Everest "because it is there" (his response to a question asked during one of his talks). Mountain climbing is a recognizable pastime the world over, though not uniformly so, since some parts of the planet are quite flat.

Mountain climbing of the nontechnical variety includes hiking, with or without a trail, to the summit, possibly "scrambling" over rocks and up low cliffs (with natural hand holds) neither steep nor high enough to call for the safety of rope. With technical climbing the terrain is more difficult, requiring rope and other specialized equipment to negotiate it. This is mountaineering, or alpine climbing, one of the subjects of this chapter and this book. Mountaineers often do some nontechnical mountain hiking just to reach the point such as a cliff face – known as "the approach" – where they will then need equipment. The technical climb as a route to the summit is, however, their principal interest.

Indeed, the types of mountain climbing beyond the scrambling level have proliferated considerably over the years, such that, presently, veterans in the field do not always agree on what they are or how to define them. Scott (2000, p. 391), for example, writes that "where once there was only one type of climber, there are now devotees of sport climbing, gym climbing, competition climbing, waterfall ice climbing, big wall climbing, alpine climbing, and high altitude climbing." *Sport climbing* stresses the technical difficulty of the moves, while, thanks to a top rope and possibly other devices, eliminating all physical risk. It is practiced on small cliffs or on indoor walls, thereby avoiding many of the problematic conditions (e.g., weather, rockfalls, long approaches) mountaineers encounter in some other types of climbing.

Some mountaineers occasionally engage in *free climbing*, or unsupported ascent of a rock face using fingers and toes (in special shoes) to grip cracks, edges, and the like. Rope, nuts, pitons, and so on, if used at all, are used only as protection against falling, not for resting or advancing up the face. This type contrasts with *aided climbing*, which relies on nuts, camming units and pitons for ascending, and rope and pulleys for descending. Traditional climbing is aided in that, here, climbers place their own protective "gear" as they ascend the mountain. Traditional climbing is sometimes referred to as *multi-pitch climbing*, so called because several lengths of rope (pitches) are needed to reach the top, whereas cragging, rock climbing, sport climbing, and the like tend to be single-pitch.

Rock climbing, sometimes, and *ice climbing*, always, are also technical pursuits, the object of which is not necessarily to arrive at a summit, but rather to climb a boulder, stretch of vertical rock, or frozen water falls. Rock climbing using a rope secured at the top of the face or bolts secured along the way is sometimes referred to as sport climbing, while cragging refers generally to climbing at a cliff area. Thus cragging can be sport climbing or climbing in a crack or both. In *bouldering*, a nontechnical form of rock climbing, climbers try, without equipment, to mount a large boulder, though they may place a mat below to cushion a fall of a short distance.

Apropos the question of risk, Heywood (1994) observes that, following its sport counterpart, there is a trend in traditional climbing toward secure movement during ascent and descent. This, however, is happening not through greater use of bolts and top roping (which would contradict the definition of traditional climbing), but through greater reliance on detailed guidebooks, training regimes, and technologically advanced equipment. Jackie Kiewa explains how this development has created tension among traditional climbers:

> Climbing has been depicted as a form of escape from the malaise affecting the modern world: a high level of predictability and consumerist orientation that creates an unprecedented standard of living at the cost of personal freedom and spontaneity. However, to retain the characteristic of resistance to this safe, comfortable and seductive society, climbers must continue to choose methods of climbing that oppose this society. They must continue to embrace uncertainty and insecurity, refuse fame or any form of hierarchy, and commit themselves to climbing for the long learning skills rather than using equipment to achieve results. Not all climbers have chosen such methods, and the resultant schism amongst climbers has led to a number of consequences. (Kiewa, 2002, p. 159)

Here is further evidence of something mentioned earlier: how pressure to conform to group goals and standards can increase the participants sense of risk.

Mountaineering

Mountaineering, as opposed to climbing mountains for reasons other than leisure, is of relative recent origin. Moreover, even the early recreational ascents were inspired not only by leisure motives but also by others, many of them scientific. Thus Horace Bénédict de Saussure, who in 1786 succeeded in the world's first technical climb (of Mt. Blanc, Switzerland), spent four and one-half hours on the summit making scientific observations and conducting experiments (Mitchell, 1983, pp. 147-148). This feat kicked off a series of expeditions organized to make first ascents of world-famous mountains, which is how the history of the sport is often presented. Today, that history is augmented with ascents of previously scaled mountains using untried routes. In nearly all cases equipment of some kind is needed to reach the top.

Many of the most challenging mountains exist in the Himalayas of Central Asia, which contain many of the world's highest peaks. In 1953 New Zealand climber Sir Edmund Hillary and Tenzing Norgay (a Sherpa) made the first successful ascent of the world's highest mountain, the Himalayan peak of Mount Everest. They led the tenth British expedition organized to tackle this challenge, the first having been led in 1921 by Mallory. A year later Italian mountaineers Achille Compagnoni and Lino Lacedelli ascended the world's second highest mountain, K2, also in the Himalayas.

As more of the world's highest mountains in Europe, Asia, and South and North America were climbed for the first time, mountaineers sought challenge in climbing ever more difficult routes and in climbing with less assistance from climbing partners. For example, Mountaineers Reinhold Messner from Italy and Peter Habeler from Austria became, in 1978, the first to scale Everest without bottled oxygen. Two years later Messner returned to successfully climb Everest entirely alone and without oxygen. Ascents became even more daring during the 1980s and 1990s, when various climbers attempted to ascend different series of related summits. In 1985 American Dick Bass became the first mountaineer to climb the highest mountain on each of the seven continents, known together as the Seven Summits, though Canadian Pat Morrow is said to have been the first to have accomplished this without guides (for details on this dispute over records, see Scott, 2000, pp. 386-387). In 1986 Messner finally completed his goal of climbing the 14 highest mountains in the world, a project that lasted 17 years. All – located in Nepal, Pakistan, China, and Tibet – are higher than eight thousand metres (26, 247 ft).

In recent years, well-publicized successes and tragedies in mountaineering as well as improvements in climbing equipment, have given rise to an increased number of mountain climbers across the world. *The Economist* (2001a, p. 39), for instance, reported that nearly 40 people ascended Everest in one week in late May, 2001, and that climbers, jostling one another as they come and go from the summit, are occasionally having to line up to cross narrow ridges. The sport's popularity has led some countries to require mountaineers to purchase climbing permits. Himalayan expeditions must also pay an environmental bond, guaranteeing that, at the end of their trip, they will remove all their waste. Indeed, all popular climbing areas are now subject to litter and the continuing presence of human-made marks and devices for guiding and aiding climbers, a situation that has given rise to a range of volunteer services.

According to Webster (2001) indoor rock climbing facilities have, since the 1980s, played an important role in introducing large numbers of people to climbing, albeit in controlled settings offering only short climbs. Still, in many ways, these conditions are artificial. Different skills and judgment are often required outdoors, because real cliffs are subject to bad weather and other hazards like loose rock and falling stones.

Such popularity has led climbing in new directions. For instance, in the late twentieth century, climbing competitions became popular with rock climbers and ice climbers of all ages and skill levels. Regular competition climbing is judged on how high the climber can ascend within a specified period of time. Speed climbing competitions pit climbers against a clock to measure how fast they can scale a wall. Local climbing gyms and clubs sponsor competitions, as do national organizations such as the American Sport Climbing Federation. Once there is competition these hobbies are transformed into sports.

In official international competitions, mountaineers, ice climbers, and rock climbers are guided on the matter of standards by the Union Internationale des Associations d'Alpinisme (UIAA). Since its founding in 1932, the UIAA has grown to represent about 80 associations in about 60 countries. As mountain climbing's popularity rose dramatically in the 1980s and 1990s, the UIAA's role in mountain safety, education, and environmental policy also increased. It also publishes a six-class system of difficulty and seven-level rating system for commitment to climbing as well as ski maps and advice for hikers. The Sierra Club (including the Sierra Club of Canada) serves a North American climbing clientele and the United States has its Alpine Club, while its counterpart in Canada is known as the Alpine Club of Canada. These organizations, along with several others that are local or regional, though essentially clubs, nevertheless occasionally address themselves to some of the same issues as UIAA. Moreover, they also offer instructional programs in climbing and provide opportunities to meet like-minded enthusiasts. Furthermore, the sample in this study suggests that by no means do all mountaineers belong to any of these entities or are otherwise formally organized.

The classification list on the following page is a truncated version of the six-class Sierra Club rating system published in Mitchell's study (1983, pp. 89-90). My intent here is to give an idea what the core activity of mountaineering actually looks like, and not to provide a technical description for climbers. Such would require much more detail, including addition of the many subdivisions within the more advanced classes.

The mountain climbing discussed in this book ranges between Classes 4 and 6, though to reach the approach (starting point of the planned ascent), climbing of the sort set out in Classes 1-3 variety may also be required.

Class 1

Cross-country hiking. Hands not needed.

Class 2

Scrambling, using hands for balance. Rope not usually necessary or desired.

Class 3

Easy climbing. . . . Rope may be desired and important for safety of less experienced climbers. . . . Handholds and footholds are necessary.

Class 4

Roped climbing with belaying. Ropes will be used by almost all party members.

Class 5

Roped climbing with protection. The leader's progress is safeguarded by the placement of intermediate points of anchorage to the mountain between the belayer and the next belay point.

Class 6

Direct aid. Upward progress is made by using chocks, pitons, slings, and other devices as handholds and footholds.

Kayaking

Kayaking is generally classified as a form of canoeing, a sport practiced in small crafts pointed at both ends. Most canoes are open-topped boats, whereas kayaks are completely enclosed except for an opening for its occupants. Both types of boats are paddled by one or more persons facing the front of the craft. Canoeists propel their boats through the water with a paddle, consisting of a wooden, aluminum, or fiberglass shaft topped with a T-shaped handle. The bottom of the shaft consists of a thin, flat blade. The canoeist holds the paddle shaft just above the blade with one hand, while the other hand grips the handle. To paddle, canoeists sit or kneel on one knee in the canoe. They then dip the paddle blade into the water, slightly ahead of the body and pull on the lower portion of the shaft while pushing on the top handle. This motion, called a "stroke," moves the boat forward. Upon completing a stroke, the canoeist pulls the blade out of the water, swings it forward, and dips it again, starting thus another stroke.

Kayak paddles have a slightly curved or spoon-shaped blade at each end of the shaft. The flat surfaces of the two blades are positioned at a right angle to one another, so that the paddler does not have to twist the paddle when executing strokes. To paddle, kayakers sit in their boats and grip the shaft, with hands equidistant from the center of the paddle. One blade is dipped into the water slightly ahead of the kayaker's body. The kayaker pulls on the shaft with the hand nearest that blade, propelling the boat forward. After finishing a stroke, the kayaker lifts the blade out of the water, simultaneously dipping the other blade into the water and pulling with the other hand. In continuing with this motion, the kayak moves forward and stays on a straight course.

Many an outdoor enthusiast enjoys canoeing or kayaking, and sometimes both, as a hobby carried out on ponds, lakes, rivers, and even relatively calm coastal sections of the sea. Some people use canoes and kayaks in conjunction with camping and fishing trips, travelling across bodies of water to remote locations. In these vessels they carry such supplies as food, tents, and sleeping bags. The Boundary Waters Canoe Area Wilderness and Voyageurs National Park, both located along the border between Minnesota and Ontario, number among the most heavily patronized canoeing areas in North America.

Wild water canoeing and kayaking on rivers with strong currents is also popular. The sections of these rivers holding greatest interest for hobbyists in this field are sometimes referred to as "whitewater," aptly named for the bubbling foam created when fast-moving water spills over and around rocks or other obstructions. Whitewater enthusiasts manoeuvre their boats around rocks, logjams, and other natural obstacles. If the current and obstacles make a passage too difficult to navigate, a canoeist (and more rarely a kayaker) may portage, that is carry the canoe over land for a short distance thereby circumventing the danger. The following history of kayaking concentrates mainly on that done on creeks and rivers (the principal interest of the kayakers of this study), some of which offer challenging wild water.

History

Canoes and kayaks have been used for travel and transportation for hundreds of years by indigenous peoples of diverse cultures. Originally, these boats, which ran in length from three to 30 feet, were built from such materials as wood, which was covered with bark; or whalebone, which was covered with animal skins. Some canoes are hollowed out logs. These vessels were used for basic transportation, trade, and in some instances, for war, and as such could be either primitively or elegantly constructed. Today most are likely to be constructed from molded plastic and fiberglass, aluminum alloys, or other synthetic materials.

The sport or hobby of canoeing is not associated with indigenous cultures. Rather "it is a recent product of nineteenth century industrial society, when an emerging middle class with wealth, sufficient to engage in leisure activities, sought out a variety of physical pastimes, which today might be referred to as recreation or when taken to an extreme, as sport" (International Canoe Federation, 2003). The modern decked canoe first appeared in the lower Thames River in Britain in the late 1850s or early 1860s. Its model was the decked canoe used by native peoples, from the Bering Sea across the Canadian Arctic to Greenland. Canadian Inuit called it a "kayak" and that is how it has come to be known throughout the industrialized world.

John MacGregor, a Scottish barrister, had a wooden kayak built in 1865, which was propelled using a traditional double bladed paddle and a light "portable" mast and sail. He was the first to organize a kayaking competition, which was sponsored by the Canoe Club at Richmond, which he founded in 1866 in Surrey, England. From that date, both racing and touring grew rapidly in popularity.

Meanwhile, in North America, the decked sailing/paddling canoe was challenged by a simpler craft: the open canoe built from birch bark, white cedar, spruce root, and gum, materials conveniently available throughout the mixed forest regions of central and eastern Canada. Used by early explorers and settlers, it was the model used for the design of elegant log canoes, which in turn, became molds for the more durable and rugged, wood plank canoe. By the 1870s these smooth-skinned craft were being turned out in numbers in boat building shops in the Peterborough region of central Canada. By this point they had become the requisite craft for anyone wishing to travel the Canadian wilderness.

The International Canoe Federation, the sport's governing body, was established in 1924. This organization, which is presently located in Budapest, Hungary, establishes standards and procedures and organizes numerous competitions around the world. The Canadian Canoe Association (CCA) is part of this federation. The CCA, among its other functions, organizes competitions and serves as a public relations source for canoeing and kayaking. It was the American Whitewater Association (2003), however, that established and disseminated the following six-fold classification of levels of difficulty for navigating rivers and creeks.

Six Classes of Difficulty

Class I

Easy. Fast moving water with riffles and small waves. Few obstructions, all obvious and easily missed with little training.

Class II

Novice. Straightforward rapids with wide, clear channels, which are evident without scouting. Occasional maneuvering may be required, but rocks and medium sized waves are easily missed by paddlers.

Class III

Intermediate. Rapids with moderate, irregular waves, which may be difficult to avoid and which can swamp an open canoe. Complex maneuvers in fast current and good boat control in tight passages or around ledges are often required; large waves and strainers may be present but are easily avoided. [A strainer is an obstruction that permits the current to flow through while filtering out solid objects.]

Class IV

Advanced. Intense, powerful but predictable rapids requiring precise boat handling in turbulent water. Depending on the character of the river, it may feature large, unavoidable waves, holes, or constricted passages demanding fast maneuvers under pressure.

Class V

Expert. Extremely long, obstructed, or very violent rapids which expose a paddler to added risk. Drops may contain large, unavoidable waves and holes or steep, congested chutes with complete demanding routes. Rapids may continue for long distances between pools, demanding a high level of fitness.

Class VI

Extreme and Exploratory. These runs have almost never been attempted and often exemplify extremes of difficulty, unpredictability and danger. The consequences of errors are very severe and rescue may be impossible.

Subdivisions exists for Classes IV and V. And, as earlier for mountain climbing, this is a summary of the actual published system of difficulty, presented here to convey a sense of the nature of the core activity. Respondents in the present study ranged from novice to expert.

Competition

Canoeing debuted at the 1924 Olympic Games in Paris as a demonstration sport, that is, as an event not officially part of the Olympic program. Not long afterward it became a popular sport in Europe, with the result that at the 1936 Olympics in Berlin, sprint canoeing and kayaking were offered as medal sports, as official Olympic events. They have been part of the Olympic sporting program since. Slalom and wild water canoeing and kayaking were developed in the 1930s as well, and slalom canoeing and kayaking gained medal status at the Olympics of 1972, 1992, 1996, and 2000. Sprint world championships were first held in 1938 in Vaxholm, Sweden, and then annually from 1970, with the exception of Olympic years. Slalom world championships have been held every two years since 1949, when they were held in Geneva, Switzerland, and wild water championships have been held every two years since 1959, when they were held in Treignac, France. The strongest national teams have traditionally come from Europe, with Germany, Sweden, Norway, Hungary, the former Yugoslavia, the former Union of Soviet Socialist Republics, France, and Italy garnering greatest success. The United States is recognized as a leading competitor in the slalom races.

In sprint canoeing and kayaking, races on still, or "flat," water are contested between individuals and teams paddling in a straight line over distances of 500 metres, 547 yards, or 1,000 metres, 1,094 yards. Slalom races are timed competitions held on a course of river rapids having a maximum length of 600 metres, or 656 yards, and through a series of 25 gates suspended over the water. If a competitor commits a fault in negotiating the course, such as touching or missing a gate, a certain number of seconds are added to the final time as a penalty. Wild water races are timed competitions contested on courses of swift, turbulent water with natural and artificial hazards. Wild water courses are at least 3 kilometres, or 1.9 miles, long. Races in all three disciplines are designated by "C" for canoes and "K" for kayak, followed by a figure indicating the number of people in the boat, for example, C1, C2, C4, K1, K2, K4. Many kayakers both race and negotiate natural challenges, leading to their dual hobbyist classification here as activity participant and sports competitor.

Snowboarding

Snowboarding, which has been described as "surfing on snow," involves an individual descending a snow-covered slope while standing sideways on a lightweight board about 150 centimetres long (about 5 feet) attached to the feet. It borrows techniques and tricks from surfing and skateboarding, and can be done wherever alpine skiing is possible. Since no poles are used in snowboarding, it is difficult to traverse flat areas. Instead, the ideal terrain is a slope covered in deep, loose snow. However ideal the slope, some snowboarders get fulfillment simply from successfully riding down it, whereas others also attempt various "tricks" en route to the bottom.

Most winter resorts now have special areas for snowboarding known as rails, half-pipes and snowboard parks. The rails, which may be placed in a larger snowboard park, are sturdy metal tubes in various shapes, which boarders attempt to ride for some distance along their length. Half-pipes – they, too, may be built as part of a snowboard park – are long, deep trenches dug in the snow and shaped like a pipe cut in half along its length. Riders "drop in" the pipe, which they accomplish by using the walls of the trench to launch themselves into the air and perform a variety of jumps and spins. Snowboard parks consist of easy to intermediate slopes augmented with a variety of bumps, jumps, gaps, and other features that riders use for jumping, or "getting air," and performing tricks. The tricks range from riding backwards, called "riding fakie," to spectacular spins and flips performed wherever terrain allows.

Unlike skiers, who shift their weight from ski to ski, snowboarders shift their weight from heels to toes as well as from one end of the board to the other. When snowboarders shift their weight toward the nose, or front of the board, the board heads downhill. When they shift their weight toward the tail, or back of the board, they head uphill or slow down. Riders execute quick turns by pulling the back foot forward or pushing it backward to change direction. They can stop the board's motion by pressing heels or toes down hard, thus digging the edge of the board into the snow.

Snowboarding requires a board, some bindings, and a pair of boots, as well as clothing suitable for the weather of the day. There are three basic types of board: freestyle, carving, and freeride (also called freecarve or all-mountain). Freestyle boards are the shortest and widest of the snowboards; they are designed to facilitate turning and the execution of tricks. They have twin tips, a design in which both ends of the board turn up slightly, much like the tip of a ski, to enable both forward and backward travel. Carving boards are longer and stiffer than freestyle boards and are directional (made to travel predominantly in one direction). Moreover, because they are narrower at the centre of the board than freestyle boards, they carve turns more easily. They also perform well on hard or icy slopes. Most freeride boards are also directional. They fall between freestyle and carving boards with reference to stiffness, length, and turning capacity, and perform well in a variety of snow conditions.

Snowboard lengths vary according to size of rider and type of riding that person does. Adult boards range in length from about 140 to 180 centimetres, or from about 4 feet 7 inches to 5 feet 11 inches. Freestyle boards are shortest, thereby giving easy maneuverability. Freeride boards are medium length, with carving boards being still longer, designed as they are to handle high speeds. Longest are the Alpine race boards, which may run up to 190 centimetres, or approximately 6 feet 3 inches. Riders use a variety of bindings to hold their boots in place on the board, including metal fasteners, plastic straps, and step-in clamps. Bindings with high backs behind the heels provide support and added leverage on turns.

History

This hobby originated in the United States between the late 1960s and early 1970s. Its popularity grew rapidly in the 1980s and 1990s, in part because it is easy to learn. Most riders attain a degree of proficiency after only a few sessions of instruction. The sense of freedom the sport offers in equipment and technique adds greatly to its appeal.

Snowboarding was developed independently by three Americans: Tom Sims, Jake Burton Carpenter, and Dimitrije Milovich. Sims is often credited with building the first snowboard, when in 1963, he modified a skateboard to slide on snow, an idea influenced in part by his experience as a surfer. Carpenter tinkered in the late 1960s with a snow toy to which he gave the name "Snurfer" (it even had a rope attached at the front) and only later realized how ski technology could improve snowboarding. Milovich, an East Coast surfer, got his inspiration from sliding on snow on cafeteria trays and based his snowboard designs on surfboards.

Snowboarding appealed initially to a small group of surfers, skateboarders, and backcountry enthusiasts. Then three factors helped popularize the sport during the 1980s (Mckhann, 2001). First, materials and technology borrowed from ski manufacturing made it easier to ride on snow. For example, manufacturers, to facilitate turning, added metal edges and produced snowboards with narrower centers. Second, a skateboard revival in the 1980s helped popularize snowboarding, when skateboarders took it up as a winter alternative. Third, ski areas began to accept snowboarders. In 1983, less than ten percent of American ski areas allowed snowboarding, but by 1997 very few of them prohibited it.

Competition

The first competitive snowboarding event was a small contest organized in 1981 in Leadville, Colorado. The following year the first National Snowboarding Championships were held at Suicide Six in Woodstock, Vermont. In 1985 the World Snowboarding Championships were launched in Lake Tahoe, California. The Fédération Internationale de ski (FIS) now holds world championships annually, while the Vancouver-based International Snowboard Federation (ISF) holds biannually a separate event, also called world championships. In 1986 Europeans began organizing regional events. The ISF held its first World Championships in 1993. Nevertheless, this organization ceased to exist in 2002, a victim of financial problems, leaving to its rival, the FIS, the responsibility of organizing all international competitions in snowboarding.

Thus, until the demise of the ISF, it and the FIS governed all world-scale snowboarding competition. The ISF was founded in 1991. In 1994 the FIS, the international governing body for skiing, recognized snowboarding as a discipline, and launched a World Cup tour, the highest level of amateur competition. In 1995 the organizers of the 1998 Nagano Winter Olympic Games announced their decision to include giant slalom (an Alpine racing event) and half-pipe snowboarding events. National bodies affiliated with either (until recently) ISF or FIS also hold competitions.

Most snowboarding competitions consist of both Alpine races and freestyle events. Alpine races resemble Alpine skiing events: A racer must navigate through a series of gates set on a hill, with the winner being the one showing the fastest time. Over the years the number of races offered at the main competitions has multiplied, so that, today, when within the jurisdiction of the FIS, riders can choose from seven: slalom, parallel slalom, giant slalom, parallel giant slalom, super giant slalom, half-pipe, snowboard cross, and special (freestyle) events. These vary, among other ways, according to how close together the gates are set.

Half-pipe, the most popular freestyle event, takes place in a huge snow trough. Competitors perform tricks, which are judged by height, landings, difficulty, and other criteria. Other snowboarding events include boardercross and slopestyle. Boardercross combines aspects of freestyle and Alpine racing. Groups of four to six riders start together and navigate a giant slalom course with banked turns, jumps, and other obstacles. Extra points are given for stunt-jumps along the way. The first two or three finishers advance to the next round until a winner is declared. Slopestyle is similar to half-pipe, but is performed in a snowboard park.

Contests not sanctioned by either the ISF or the FIS often feature showier events, such as "Big Air" competitions. Music is often an important accompaniment to these. The World Extreme Snowboarding Championships, held annually in Valdez, Alaska, is an unsanctioned event. In extreme contests, snowboarders roar through narrow chutes, over steep drop-offs, and across other kinds of difficult terrain.

As for a formal system of course difficulty, such as found in kayaking and mountaineering, the one used in snowboarding is comparatively simple. In the Canmore-Banff area it is the four-class scale posted on the runs, or trails, of the alpine ski hills on which the snowboarders also ride:

Green circle: novice run

Blue square: intermediate run

Black diamond: advanced run

Double black diamond: super-advanced run

As the level of required expertise rises, the run gets steeper with more turns and more advanced moguls (bumps of snow) to negotiate. Back-country snowboarding, like cross-county skiing, has no classification system.

Conclusions

One might get the impression from reading this chapter that the three activities discussed here, especially kayaking and snowboarding, are more sport than rule-based participation (the nonsport type of physically active hobby, see Chapter 2). If our samples are typical, however, this conclusion is invalid. The large majority of interviewees spoke of the thrill and fulfillment they gained from trying to meet natural challenges through their hobby, and said that competing with other people while trying to do this was by no means always their idea of the most exciting use of their free time.

The leisure careers of these hobbyists are thus, for most of them, founded on moving up in the classification system of their pursuit, rather than entering and winning competitions in it. They see themselves as getting better at what they love to do (and come to love it even more as a result of improvement). But there is more to a career than this. For they also see their leisure careers as unfolding along lines of accumulating experience, both in terms of number of seasons in the hobby and in terms of significant places they have climbed, kayaked, or snowboarded. It is not just climbing mountains or paddling rivers, in general, but rather climbing particular mountains and paddling particular rivers known in hobbyist circles for their celebrated natural challenges. Competitors add to this career base by participating in and, if all goes well, winning at recognized contests. But everyone in these samples was first and foremost a hobbyist challenging nature, with a few of them supplementing this approach by adding the sporting element of contest.

Chapter 4

Leisure Careers

The desire of knowledge, like the thirst of riches,
increases ever with the acquisition of it.

Laurence Sterne
Tristram Shandy, **Book II, chap. 3 [1760]**

Exploratory research on careers in serious leisure has so far proceeded from a broad, rather loose definition: a leisure career is the typical course, or passage, of a type of amateur, hobbyist, or volunteer that carries the person into and through a leisure role, and possibly, into and through a work role. The essence of any career, whether in work, leisure, or another area of life, lies in the temporal continuity of the activities associated with it. Moreover, we are accustomed to thinking of this continuity as one of accumulating knowledge, experience, skill, and prestige, as progress along these lines from some starting point, even though continuity may also include career retrogression. In the worlds of sport and entertainment, for instance, athletes and artists may reach performance peaks in early adulthood, after which prestige and rewards diminish as the limelight shifts to younger, sometimes more capable practitioners. Serious leisure careers have been empirically examined and substantiated in my own research (for a partial summary see Stebbins, 1992, chap. 5), the research of Baldwin and Norris (1999), and that of others (see Stebbins, 2001a, p. 124).

Career continuity may occur predominantly within, between, or outside organizations. Careers in organizations such as a community orchestra or hobbyist association only rarely involve the challenge of "bureaucratic crawl," to use C. Wright Mills's imagery. In other words, little or no hierarchy exists for people to climb. Nevertheless, amateurs and hobbyists still gain a profound sense of continuity, and hence career, from their more or less steady development as skilled, experienced, and knowledgeable participants in particular forms of serious leisure and from their deepening satisfaction that accompanies this kind of personal growth. Some volunteer careers are intraorganizational as well.

Still, many amateurs and volunteers, along with some hobbyists, have careers that bridge two or more organizations. For them, career continuity stems from a growing reputation as skilled, knowledgeable practitioners and, based on this estimation, from finding increasingly better leisure opportunities available through various outlets (as in different teams, orchestras, organizations, tournaments, exhibitions, journals, conferences, contests, shows, and the like). Meanwhile, still other amateurs and hobbyists, who pursue noncollective lines of leisure (e.g., tennis, painting, clownery, golf, entertainment magic), are free of even this marginal affiliation with an organization. The extraorganizational career of the informal volunteer, the forever willing and sometimes highly skilled and knowledgeable helper of friends, relatives, and neighbors is of this third type. The hobbyists of this study have, for the most part, extraorganizational leisure careers.

Serious leisure participants who stick with their activities eventually pass through four, possibly five career stages: beginning, development, establishment, maintenance, and decline. But the boundaries separating these stages may be imprecise in some fields, for as the condition of continuity suggests, participants in them pass almost imperceptibly from one to the next. The beginning lasts as long as is necessary for interest in the activity to take root. Development begins after the interest has taken root and its pursuit becomes more or less routine and systematic. Serious leisure participants advance to the establishment stage once they have moved beyond the requirement of having to learn the basics of their activity. During the maintenance stage, the leisure career is in full bloom; here participants are now able to enjoy to the utmost their pursuit of it, the uncertainties of getting established having, for the most part, been put behind them. Toward career's end some, though by no means all, serious leisure participants face decline. Those who do, experience it because of deteriorating mental or physical skills. A more detailed description of the career framework and its five stages is available elsewhere (Stebbins, 1992, chap. 5; on hobbies see Stebbins, 1996a).

Beginning

In general, beginning a leisure career in these hobbies is a social affair, as evidenced below, something accomplished in the company of others. This generalization holds for both male and female participants, even if in climbing, the people involved with the neophyte sometimes varied by sex.

Mountain climbers enter their hobby in one of three ways, all of them involving other people and all more or less equally common with this sample. One way is to meet by chance one or a handful of climbers. For instance, a male respondent started conversing with a couple of climbers while all three were rafting together. A woman got into climbing through a new boyfriend. Another way is take an adult education course exclusively on climbing or on climbing and related outdoor activities. The third way, which may also be part of the second, is to go to a climbing gym, initial interest in the hobby having already been kindled by, say, films or magazines. Here the novice gets basic instruction and some rudimentary experience. Still, some climbers get started informally, through a sort of on-the-job training from more experienced practitioners, which they usually augment with some self-directed reading. In all these instances climbers begin their hobby in a social setting.

As for age of start-up, the snowboarders launched their careers much earlier in life than the other two, taking up their hobby at a mean age of 12, compared with the mean starting age of 18 and 19 for the climbers and the kayakers.

Consonant with the social basis of entry into climbing, all but one of this subsample mentioned a friend or two, or much more rarely, a relative who was instrumental in their choosing this hobby. Only one respondent found initial impetus in isolation from others, in her case, watching films on mountain climbing. Whether male or female, the sources of early inspiration were highly likely to be male, and for females the man was typically a boyfriend.

The two most common approaches of taking up whitewater kayaking were also social. One approach was to satisfy curiosity by enrolling in a course, usually several days long, whereas another was to see kayakers in action and desire to get in on the fun. Sometimes the kayakers being observed were friends, sometimes they were strangers observed while the respondent was rafting. Whichever way, it was, for this activity, love at first sight. Thus, a female interviewee described her first time in a kayak:

> First week I went up the Red Deer [river] and they took a canoe for me and nobody wanted to paddle with me, everybody wanted to be in a kayak so they threw me in a kayak and I made it down without tipping and it was just the biggest rush, I loved it. I had a bit of an advantage because I can read the water from my canoeing experience. I felt secure on the water.

A male kayaker had a similar initial experience:

> I liked it. It was fun; it was a thrill. First off it was really challenging because I just kept rolling over all the time. It seemed very natural because I had very much a water background, done a lot of sailing and used to have a cabin at the lake when I was young.

A couple of respondents had a more gradual initiation into the hobby, namely, encountering it as one of a set of activities available at a children's summer camp. Entering the hobby as a loner through self-instruction, at least as far as this sample is concerned, is rare; only one person said this is how he began his kayaking career.

The vast majority of kayakers took up their hobby through encouragement of a friend or, not wanting to enter alone, through persuading a friend to join them. Often this was accomplished by going together for kayaking lessons or to rent a boat to try out on a local lake or river. Three respondents, however, said they approached the hobby alone, inspired entirely by indirect sources. And nearly all the respondents had been on the water before they took up kayaking, primarily in a canoe, but for a minority, in a raft.

For nearly all the snowboarders, entry started with watching someone else do the hobby or seeing it done in pictures (e.g., video, magazine) that piqued their curiosity to try it themselves. Most of these neophytes had been downhill skiers or skateboarders, if not both, so snowboarding appeared to them as an interesting extension of these activities. Old snowboarders did not see snowboarding on the ski hill, however, for in its early days, this new and upstart hobby was unwelcome there. They were more likely than younger snowboarders to have become interested through such media as film and magazines. Even more than the first two groups, the snowboarders were encouraged to take up the hobby by friends, or somewhat more rarely, by one or more relatives. In fact, none of this sample got into it strictly alone. A few in the sample had also surfed before getting into skateboarding, but growing up inland, as happened with the majority of interviewees in this study, they found scant opportunity to experiment with this activity.

Increasing Involvement

As mentioned the stages of a leisure career can be imprecise, which once a start was made, was certainly true in these three hobbies. Accordingly, in this section, we will examine, without always identifying each stage along the way, the hobbyist's increasing involvement, as it subtly evolves from development through to maintenance.

Most of the climbers, once they discovered their passion for their pursuit, plunged abruptly into the development stage with great enthusiasm, heading out whenever their work and domestic schedules permitted. For many this meant weekend climbs within driving distance from home, which was usually in the town of Canmore located just outside the main gate to the east side of Banff National Park. Some, however, climbed more frequently having arranged their employment such that they had the climbing season free. Alternatively, these devotees would take "expeditions," climbing trips to distant parts of the world such as Tibet, Nepal, or South America. And others climbed a great deal throughout the week, but as often as not, in a climbing gym.

A smaller number of climbers took up their hobby more gradually. Over the years they became progressively more involved, climbing more, climbing farther, and taking longer climbing trips. This group tended to have one or two other serious leisure activities that they pursued during the same season and that commanded at least equal attention. Sometimes this gradual involvement was given a boost by joining a climbing club. At other times it hinged on meeting certain people. For example, a couple of female climbers noted that their climbing interests tended to change to match those of their current boyfriend.

For the entire sample the goal was always to try to develop: to get better at the activity, to become stronger, to learn more about the kind of climbing the participant preferred, and for some though not all, to advance to more sophisticated forms such as progressing from Class 3 to Class 4 or from Class 4 to Class 5. Many of the sample also spoke of being "pushed" by better climbers they had come to know to tackle more challenging, though not usually significantly more risky, routes and forms of climbing.

Given this orientation to the hobby, this sample saw climbing competitions as by and large insignificant in their leisure careers. Most of them had never competed, and for those who did, the competitions were infrequent and regarded as side interests. One male said of competitions:

> [I] wasn't really . . . [I was] pretty put off by the whole thing actually. Nothing about the sponsors . . . it was more what I saw in myself, I guess. Like for a couple [of competitions] there, I felt really confident and really strong or whatever and just sort of got into it with no expectations, cause nobody knew who you were and stuff like that and then . . . it's like, oh I don't know if I can do it. . . . You start getting all these outside pressures, and then I'm not climbing because I think of it as fun, I'm climbing because . . . I should. . . . But to me I always want climbing to be fun, and I realized that I wasn't having that much fun anymore. I guess I just stopped.

The opposite pattern of development in their leisure career was observed for the kayakers. Most started gradually, while a much smaller number started abruptly, with more or less the same level of intense participation. In kayaking, as in mountain climbing, no notable gender differences in the development patterns were observed.

The lengthy technical preparation for meeting this nature challenge of kayaking partly accounts for the tendency of a gradual pattern of development. Critical to experiencing fulfillment in river kayaking is learning to "roll," to be able to right one's self when the boat capsizes. This manoeuvre and others done with the double-bladed paddle were most commonly learned through some sort of instruction, usually in a formal course, but sometimes in an informal series of lessons received from a friend or relative. Those who do not know how to roll must know how to swim, for the latter is the only alternative when the kayak flips over. Neophytes in kayaking are marked as learners by, among other qualities, their frequent "swims." Some are further marked by a fear of rushing water, which must be overcome before they will participate frequently and with ease. A male kayaker explained why the learning period tends to be long:

It has rather a steep learning curve. It takes about a year to sort of get over that hump, a year if everything is going well. So until you get over the hump, it never actually becomes enjoyable. I shouldn't say that cause I enjoyed it right from the beginning, and some people do, but some people hate it. If you can get over that hump . . . take Nancy [my wife] who crossed that path early last year, but her preference two years ago . . . or maybe it was almost three years ago, would have been to go mountain biking. Just last year she wanted to go kayaking, so that was a big change for her. Once you are over that hump it is an incredibly addictive sport.

White-water kayakers who enter their careers full tilt have both time and drive to master the basic kayaking skills and then move quickly to developing their speciality, be it river running, rodeo boating, slalom competitions, or creek running. And most kayakers in this sample, however long it took to get into their hobby, had a speciality, though they sometimes did other things as well. And some enjoyed entering competitions in it, whereas others were content simply to meet the challenge of the water. In many localities these specialities are practiced within the framework of a local club, which may also have provided the courses that some of the sample took (kayaking courses are also available through municipal continuing education programs).

During the season, eager kayakers, like mountain climbers, tend to pursue their hobby every free weekend. Many add to this foundation one or more special kayaking trips of a week or two in length, enabling them to cover stretches of rivers renowned for their challenge. Experienced respondents committed to the maintenance of their kayaking careers often described the level of their involvement in terms of number of days spent paddling per year (e.g., 120-130 days). They also described their career in technical terms, regardless of stage, as having developed both ability and confidence to the point of being capable of handling a particular class of river (e.g., I am a Class 4 or a Class 5 river kayaker).

Nevertheless, from the standpoint of time, not all kayaking careers are linear. Several respondents said they experienced gaps, some as long as five to eight years, during which the person was, for the most part, away from the hobby. Sometimes this was occasioned by educational demands, sometimes by relocation to a region of the country where rivers offered comparatively little challenge, sometimes by a desire for extensive travel or the irresistible appeal of another serious leisure activity. Three of the sample incurred injury while kayaking, forcing them to renounce it for a while. In a couple of instances, injury was traumatic enough to dampen interest in advancing farther up the classification scale.

The most common career development in snowboarding was characterized first by delay and hesitation, and then by intense participation. This pattern differs from the patterns of career development in kayaking and mountain climbing, which were qualified as gradual and abrupt, respectively. Furthermore, in kayaking, gender differences are evident, for males pioneered this hobby and were therefore more likely than females to develop in it according to the pattern of delay and then intense participation.

That is, this pattern in snowboarding exists in considerable part because some respondents became interested in the hobby during its early days, when commercial equipment was still in short supply (which was, in any case, poorly constructed compared with that of today) and ski hills were hostile toward the new activity. Moreover, most were still in school, and therefore often had to rely on parents and others for transportation and money for equipment and, where allowed, ski passes. These favors were by no means always forthcoming. Finally, some of the sample experienced a delay in steady snowboarding, because of competing leisure interests such as a sport or extended travel. Inconsistent snow conditions during some seasons, such as too much warm weather and, as a result, icy slopes, also limited participation.

Nonetheless, when such contingencies were absent, respondents reported an abrupt and intense development in their careers in this hobby, specifically in practice snowboarding sessions at least a couple of times a week throughout the season. However long it took for participation to reach a steady and frequent rate (maintenance), the snowboarding career advances through development and establishment with the person getting better at controlling the board, learning to do the usual manoeuvres in the park, getting skilled at riding over higher and higher cliffs, and so on. Backcountry riders must learn how to descend on ungroomed slopes, possibly under threat of avalanche. As in kayaking, major injury can seriously limit involvement in this hobby, forcing a person's career into decline, if not termination.

Some respondents fell in love with one or more types of competition, thus, at this point, turning their hobby into a sport. Slalom racing and sets of snowboard park manoeuvres (called, among other things, "jams" or "comps") number among the competitions they entered, for which there are frequently monetary prizes paid to the top competitors. At least at this time, however, accumulated earnings from these events and from sponsorships have not been sufficient to constitute a livelihood, although they can nicely offset some travel and equipment costs.

Furthermore, the sample was more or less divided on the merits of competition, even though neither gender of respondent nor level of experience were evident in this division. One male said it had no appeal.

> I did try competing for a while when I first came out to Banff, but competitions aren't for me. I would rather go out and ride backcountry or an open bowl or some chutes. I like free riding a lot more than the freestyle aspect of it, but freestyle is definitely fun, and it is definitely the up and coming thing in snowboarding. As far as competitions, I competed in two out at Lake Louise; one was a slope style, one was a half-pipe. Slope style is just a basic run with a partner, where they have fifteen jumps or eight jumps set up and you have got to go through them without falling.

A female boarder, on the other hand, cannot get enough of competitions.

> It has always been about having fun, and I always said that the minute I stop having fun snowboarding in competing then I will stop doing it, not snowboarding but stop competing. Basically I compete probably like between seven and ten races a year, just mostly provincial, and I do usually one trip, like this year I went to California and Vancouver for a race. That is basically about it, most of the days are just spent on the hill free riding and just having fun and the odd weekend between, basically January and March, is boardercrossing.

This period of increasing involvement is, in all three hobbies, also the period of greatest growth in positive commitment to the core activity. It becomes so attractive in the development and maintenance stages of the hobbyist career, that the individual wants intensely to devote ever more time, money, and energy to its pursuit, to getting better at it, and to acquiring better equipment. Obviously, most everyone faces unavoidable upper limits on reaching these desiderata, so expressing commitment along these lines can at times be frustrating. Still, no one wanted to abandon the hobby, because he or she was being thwarted in this way.

Thrills as Motivational Events

Thrills, or high points, are the sharply exciting events and occasions that stand out in the minds of those who pursue a kind of serious leisure. In general, they tend to be associated with the rewards of self-enrichment and, to a lesser extent, those of self-actualization and self-expression. That is, thrills in serious leisure may be seen as situated manifestations of the more abstract rewards; they are what hobbyists in each field seek as concrete expressions of the rewards they find there. They are important, in substantial part, because they motivate the participant to stick with the pursuit in hope of finding similar experiences again and again, and because they demonstrate that diligence and commitment can pay off.

The interviewer asked the respondents to discuss some of the thrills they had during their careers as climbers, kayakers, or snowboarders. Here, too, with a few exceptions, no noteworthy differences between men and women were discovered. Regardless of sex the mountain climbers most often cited as thrilling their ability to meet an exceptional challenge (for their level of knowledge and ability) presented by a particular rock face and nearly as often the panoramic view they beheld once on top. Meeting the challenge consisted of many elements, depending on the climb in question. In some instances it included overcoming fatigue, in others it meant overcoming fear or pushing oneself to personal limits. Conquering fear was thrilling when the perceived risk at hand gets redefined as manageably dangerous. In the words of a female climber:

> It always seems to be those moments when your life is at risk that really stand out the most I think, as a thrill. I can remember Chinaman's Peak [since renamed Ha Ling] with Chris [pseudonym] three years ago now when we were off route and we knew that two people had just died there the year before. And it was a real thrill, because I thought we pulled it off really well; we kept it together and it worked out really well and I even learned that I could push myself. I always knew that I was able to handle those kind of situations well, but I guess being in it just sort affirmed that to me.

After these experiences some respondents spoke of seeing in a different light, life in general, and themselves in particular. Another common thrill, even if it sometimes failed to offer challenges of the sort just described, was climbing for the first time, an objective that is well known in climbing circles.

Compared with the mountain climbers the kayakers experienced a wider range of thrills. The respondents discussed three, each offering in its own peculiar way challenges that, when met, contributed substantially to the thrilling experience. One frequently mentioned thrill was successfully negotiating a major drop in the river, often one high enough to qualify as a waterfall. Speaking from a different angle, a female interviewee said it is thrilling to "be in zone."

So focused on what you're doing. It is a great distraction, everything is in slow, out-of-body experience. I get giggly before a big waterfall. Part of it is tingles, not being quite sure what is going to happen. There is always the X factor (the unknown). For some of us that is a real rush, the unknown.

New challenging rivers and creeks, especially ones celebrated in kayaking circles, constitute another thrill. It is the large sections of rapids here that are particularly exhilarating to paddle. A corollary of this thrill is successfully running for the first time a river or creek on which the person had failed in the past. This second thrill was by far the most common of the three.

The third thrill comes with making a succession of good moves on a standing wave in a river, such as surfing it (riding back and forth on the downstream side of the wave) or spinning on it. The impact of the thrill is that much greater if the wave in question is renowned for its challenging qualities. Another female kayaker described her experiences in this area of the hobby.

Yeah, one was on the Thompson last year, managing to surf on these two huge waves. Not everyone could get on them, but I managed to get on and surfed them. And it was a really satisfying thing, because I paddled it well and I surfed these waves that I heard about. . . . It was kind of a landmark for me. 'Cause there were other people who didn't want to do it, so it made me feel like, yeah, I have finally arrived at a level where it's very satisfying for actually doing it and for feeling that I could do it. It was a thrill just doing the surf, because they were huge waves. And there was one this past weekend. There was just one little section on the water that I had walked around before, and I ran a very challenging section and I knew my line and I hit my line perfectly and it went fine. It was exciting, but I was also in control. That was neat, because it was a real thrill.

In river kayaking, as will also be evident for the other two hobbies, some physically dangerous, risky situations get retrospectively defined simultaneously as both a thrill and an epic. "Epics" are harrowing experiences of heroic proportions that the hobbyist manages to survive, albeit sometimes with injury.

At the time they are happening, however, these situations are unpleasant. In fact the objective in question is not successfully negotiated, but a sense of thrill is nonetheless preserved after the fact by coming out of the failed attempt relatively unscathed. In the course of it all, the kayaker, for example, had to "swim," fractured a limb on the rocks, or broke up the nose of the boat. But it could have been worse, perhaps culminating in more broken bones, even death. In some epics, kayakers are forced to leave the river in inaccessible places, with the result that colleagues must rescue them, or if the situation is perilous, as in a canyon, this task is left to professional search and rescue.

The principal thrill for snowboarders, as for many downhill skiers, is to find deep powder snow in which to ride down a challenging slope, ideally one situated in a mountain bowl. Such conditions are most consistently found at high elevation in the backcountry and on the ski slopes following a major snowfall. And this is why "heliboarding" is popular among those few who can afford to pay the airlift to the top of the mountain.

> It totally feels like you are floating, and if you stop, you would fall through, like falling through a cloud or something. It is absolutely amazing — the scenery and no one else is around — and you are there with a few friends having a great time and just the whole deal is great. And the fact that there is a danger element to it as well — [possible] avalanches — that is part of the thrill. — *female snowboarder*

Otherwise, several in the snowboarding sample mentioned as thrilling, successfully riding over ledges and cliffs, although fear is the usual sentiment when the cliff to be negotiated is unknown to the boarder.

Female snowboarders tended to be thrilled at being able to ride well in a hobby presently dominated by males. This thrill may be experienced most often in the snow parks, where contact among participants is close and quality of performance evident to everyone present. One female respondent said of her thrills in this hobby:

Probably riding park every day is one of them, cause it is nice to go out there and go as big as the guys do and have people come up to me and go "nice air buddy" and they look at you and they go "oh, nice air." They totally don't expect you to be a girl. It is just kind of good you know, like yeah, I can do it, too. In a couple of my heats in the boardercrosses, I have come in first, and that is a really good feeling 'cause you beat four other girls, and it is like, yahoo!

Although the kayakers seemed to talk the most about epics, the term and the experience it signifies, were also well recognized by both snowboarders and climbers. It is usually an epic when climbers fall a significant distance, doing so "on equipment," as opposed to falling to their death (survival is a quintessential element of the epic). Boarders riding a cliff drop can, upon landing, break limbs. As one male put it: "a cliff drop in powder where I missed a tree with my head. It was a thrill to live." A female mountaineer gave a lengthy account of an equally lengthy epic climb.

R: Yeah, this epic just about killed me. I went to climb it with a friend of mine, Randy [pseudonym], and I guess he had quite a bit more experience than I have ever had. He has done quite a few big mountains, and he is quite accomplished in what he is doing. But I guess he has never really climbed in the Rockies, and I guess now he knows — he just thought he would go ultra light, and we didn't have, like I wanted to take a first aid kit with us and he said no. I wanted to take a head torch and he said no. So we didn't have a head torch. He had one and I had one sitting at the car. He didn't even take a shell for himself. I took a shell, 'cause I refused to let him say I couldn't take a shell, but I did put my shell pants back in the car.

Right from the word go I didn't feel too great about it, 'cause I have never climbed without a head torch, the general things that I usually take. Anyway we took off, and we kind of spent a bit of time trying to find our route and we finally got on it. But it was about 1:00 or so, and we got high enough on the mountain that we could see over Mount Edith. I just saw this storm coming in, and I wasn't into it at all. I was like, you know, I think it is time we turned around, you know. And he said, yeah, I think we should — we both didn't realize how many more pitches we had to go — and he said I think we should keep going because there is a path that goes all the way down. And to go down, I would admit, would have been a bit of a pain, but I said you know with my gear I'll just buy more [sometimes it is necessary to abandon certain gear during the course of a climb].

It is not that important to me now I just want to — we had already had a great day and that is just one of the things — this was definitely not the time to be climbing on the mountain. I guess I just knew deep down that we shouldn't be there, and I let him talk me into continuing. That was something that I know now, and again if I want to continue on a mountain that somebody is uncomfortable with in my party, well then we go down. The mountain is not going anywhere; you can climb it another day. That is all it takes, if one person wants to go down, then the day should be over.

So anyway we continued, and we were about five pitches from the top and it started snowing. This storm just hit us, and the stupid thing was that we could see it coming and he just wouldn't go down. We got hit by the storm, and it wasn't really a problem. I mean the snow and the rain, and then it snowed, and the wind, and the thunder and lightening. I suppose it wasn't really a problem until about the last two pitches. I guess we just sort of dealt with it going all around us, but the lightening was getting more frequent and we were feeling it definitely through the rock. Every two minutes we were getting a charge. You would hear the mountain buzz kind of like get louder and louder, and you would get a bit of a shock. It definitely wasn't a direct hit, but you would feel a bit of a pain in your chest, your arm or your leg. And then, when we had two pitches to go, because it had been snowing for so long now, we were starting to get really cold.

I had stopped shivering, and I was starting to slur and I really couldn't put together very good sentences. I was trying to climb the last two pitches, but my hands were not, you know a full day of climbing and I had just gotten so cold. I couldn't feel down to my wrists, so it really didn't matter the pain, 'cause I couldn't feel my hands. But I couldn't get into the stick, and I just kept sliding out and I was getting — I know we had to move fast but I couldn't, we are still going. I was trying to clean a piece of gear, and I have a metal plate in my mouth and it is quite hard the lightening hit a piton and it went through my head. I wasn't getting scared, but I guess I sort of thought well I was just waiting for the one to hit me. Like I thought this is it. I thought, well, I am just going to keep climbing. I am just going to keep moving, keep going, and four times, four separate occasions on those two pitches I actually got blown off the mountain. Lightening hit, but again, I don't think it was a full hit, because it was nothing like that bad. But it actually did blow me off the mountain, and so I am like lying on the rope and I was a little dazed. And then I would come around and, oh my God I am lying on the rope. Really bad because I had no idea how good his anchor was, and I had no real idea how long I had been there. Probably only a few seconds, but I couldn't really tell. So I would get back on and start climbing.

Finally we topped out, and Jack, Linda, and this other guy Tom [all pseudonyms] were sitting at the top. Jack's partner Tom was lying upside down on the mountain, and I just didn't really know what was going on; it kind of looked a bit strange to me. I asked him what was going on. "Oh, he's dead." What the hell do you mean he's dead? What is going on, and he said he is dead. He has been hit in the head by lightening, and he is dead, [but] we got to go, you know. Anyway they [the other two climbers] climbed the whole thing, and they just kind of expected that we would rescue them and I guess, he was so concerned about himself, and didn't even really seem to give a crack about this guy that was lying on the mountain. He just assumed that he was dead. So I went over and checked on this guy, and he had a heart beat and he was breathing. All I really had to do was a sternum rub, and he came around. And anyway we asked him who he was, and he couldn't tell us anything. But just to sort of see what was happening in his brain, he thought he was on a completely different mountain when we asked him where he was. And so we knew he was pretty baked. And it was really shocking. . . .

I have never seen anything that drastic before, I have seen some people in pretty bad ways in the ocean or rafting before, but I have never really — this much going on and this intense before and somebody was ready to leave him — I had never really seen that before. Anyway, so we basically had to baby both of them down the mountain. We still had to find the anchors. And the fact that Jack had been on that mountain so many times before and had no idea where to go, so we knew pretty much that he had either been baked a little bit or he was very, very cold. So I guess we found the anchors. We just had to get down, we had to get out of this lightning range it was just getting to be all a joke. So we kept "rapping" [rappelling], having somebody belay Jack so we could stop him 'cause he could still seem to function (though he really had no idea what to do with a "biner" [carabiner]). So, anyway, we got both of them down. But like even after about the second rappel, Jack was still like "I am going to leave you," this sort of stuff. I wasn't dealing with it very well; I was getting beyond cold by this stage. I was just getting worse and worse; there was no leveling out for me once I got really cold. I just seemed to go downhill, because I wasn't exerting myself — too much time to spend — I just knew I had to keep concentrating. Focus — this whole time I am having to watch my hands 'cause I couldn't feel them. Dealing with this guy who asked me if this person could die, I was just like "will you shut up." I threatened to punch his head in, and told him I was going to put his nose on the other side of his face if he didn't shut up. I just screamed at him. And I realized there and then after I screamed at him that this isn't helping. So I made myself rappel first and made Jack the last, so that I wouldn't have too much time with him. That seemed to help just to get myself away from him, 'cause he was just driving me nuts.

Anyway, we finally got them down, and we had to get out of there. They had gear at the bottom. And I wrote down the details, and made sure that they contacted me after they had gotten both of themselves to hospital, 'cause I wanted them both to get checked out. We had to leave them. We had nothing to sleep in, and we probably could have shared sleeping bags and stuff, but at this stage we felt the car wasn't that far away and we just had to go. And Tom was doing just fine. He was rappelling by himself, he was pulling ropes. And he seemed like he was going to be just fine so. . . .

I: *So what happened when you got down?*

R: We were going to take off for the car. And of course, we were just trying to go as fast as we could. But once we got into the trees we couldn't see anything, and wandering around inside the bush wasn't really the greatest idea when we couldn't see a trail. We thought this is stupid, we are going to get lost. So we spooled the ropes out, and I lied down on top of the ropes 'cause Randy wasn't even that cold. I couldn't believe it — maybe he has just got a bigger engine than me. So we spooled the ropes out, and got inside the pack. He laid down on top of me, so that I could use his warmth.

And I just remember lying there. I don't know how long we lied there, but it was ages. I was starting to hallucinate. Like I could see flashlights, and would be, like, getting real excited like "There are people coming Randy, there are people coming." And he is, like, there is nobody there, and I would be, like, so deflated when I realized that nobody was there. And then I heard voices and footsteps and all that sort of stuff and then I realized that they weren't there again. And I remember just about going to sleep.

And I just remembered something in my head saying "Nancy [pseudonym] move, just move, you can't lie here anymore. You are not going to make it, you are going to die." So I said to Randy, I am going to die, I am not going to make it to the morning. I have got to get up and do something. I have to at least make an effort, I can't just lie here and give it up. I just got really angry, like a surge of energy. I just got really, really angry, and I just thought I am not dying, not here.

I crawled on my hands and knees so that I could feel for debris. Like there was bush over here and bush over there, and pretty much because it was a path. I thought it would be clear, so I thought if I ran into bush, I would just feel around until I could feel more path. And then when I was sure I was on the trail, I would call Jack to me. And then I would go off again and then I would call Randy to me. We got out at about 2:00 in the morning.

I: So how long a day had it been?

R: About twenty-five hours.

In short, the thrill of the epic, when described as such, comes in surviving it, an experience that all three types of hobbyists usually had no interest in repeating, however thrilling it was in retrospect. It was, after all, a harrowing brush with fortuitous risk (see Chapter 1). Be that as it may, recounting particular epics makes for great shoptalk at social gatherings of these hobbyists. In such sessions there are lessons to be learned, heroes to be identified, danger points in the hobby to be underscored, and so on. Tales of epics, no doubt embellished as they pass from mouth to mouth in such sessions, come to form a significant part of the activity's local subculture.

The Future

Everyone in the mountain climbing sample said their future included more climbing, to the point where their body will no longer take it. A female climber said: "I plan to keep climbing, and keep developing my skills, abilities, and knowledge. I don't plan on ever stopping. This is the first sport that has ever captivated me totally. It is a huge part of my life." Most interviewees also hoped for an improvement in skills and knowledge of their hobby. A few had big trips in mind, centered on famous mountains in North America or elsewhere in the world.

Likewise with the kayakers: everyone intended to stay in the hobby far into the future. Many, being still at the establishment stage, wanted to do more as well as more challenging rivers, with some of these being in other parts of North America or abroad (e.g., Nepal, South America). Many also wanted to learn new skills (a number mentioned taking up rodeo) or polish old ones. But almost an equal number said they were happy with their present level of competence in the hobby, and just wanted to continue at that level of river running. They are at the maintenance stage of their careers. Many of this latter group mentioned the increased sense of risk that would emerge should they start paddling at a more advanced class.

> Yeah. I don't think I ever want to be in a situation where I fear my life is at risk. I suppose it is just the nature of the activity; it always is there to a small degree. But I don't want to be in a situation where I fear; where I am paddling in a river where I say if I screw up here I'm in real big, big trouble. So I don't want to die kayaking, I don't want to get to that level where I am doing the stuff that definitely if you mess up you are dead.
> — *female kayaker*

A couple of respondents – one man, one woman – said having children made them more conservative in this regard.

The snowboarders to an interviewee said they would be pursuing their hobby until they physically could do it no more. As one female put it: "I just want to ride every day. I don't really care if it goes anywhere I just like being able to . . . I want to be active, to be getting out here, getting fresh air." But, unlike the climbers and kayakers, only a few snowboarders specifically mentioned trying to develop further, as in learning new tricks (e.g., jumps, spins). Rather, when there were plans other than to simply continue on doing what they have been doing, they planned to snowboard in new places such as Europe or Chile, or get into the backcountry and deep powder.

Conclusions

Most of the climbers can be said to still be in the process of establishing themselves in their hobby, in that they envisage significant future improvement in skill and knowledge. The kayakers were more evenly divided as to those who had reached maintenance and those still in establishment. The snowboarding sample had the greatest number of participants now at the maintenance stage. No one in the overall sample could be classified as being in career decline, but this simply reflects my intentional bias of sampling active hobbyists. For, in all three of these highly physical hobbies, as people age, decline becomes ever more inevitable.

Why these differences in stage of career across the three samples? The data offer a possible answer to this question, in that, as noted previously, participants enter snowboarding at a much earlier age than they do kayaking and mountain climbing. This suggests that, compared with the other two, the first have a substantial head-start in reaching establishment. They get the jump on the others in developing a realistic sense of the diverse rewards available in their pursuit and in acquiring the skill, knowledge, and experience that help make many of them so powerfully attractive.

Career, as process, is important because it constitutes a strong and continuing motivational force. For instance, both success and failure in a career often motivate people to try to build on the first to achieve still more success and to do what they can to minimize any of the second. Moreover, careers in particular roles seem to encourage at various points in time both retrospective and prospective reviews of how they have gone and how they will or could go in the future. Strategizing on what to do with reference to one's career in the present or in the future is part of this stock-taking. This is as true of leisure roles as it is of non-leisure roles. Still, this observation is probably most valid for serious leisure roles, where over the long-term, there are skills and knowledge to develop and apply, and experience to accumulate and profit from.

The motivational properties of the leisure career are intimately related to the costs and rewards experienced in the hobby, conditions that deliver their own motivational kick.

Chapter 5

Costs, Rewards, and Motivation

There is no disappointment we endure
One half so great as that we are to ourselves.

Philip James Bailey
Festus, "The Sun" [1839]

How do people view their own motives for participating in their leisure activities? The psychology of leisure needs and motivation has only recently begun to consider their point of view. In 1989, Mannell (1989, p. 286) observed that psychological research, while confirming the general existence of leisure satisfaction, had so far failed to identify "the most meaningful and appropriate factors that might affect the quality of . . . [that] satisfaction." In other words, psychologists of the day were assuming rather than empirically studying the link between leisure fulfillment, on the one hand, and the everyday life components of motivation in particular leisure activities and their settings, on the other. At the same time, they had nevertheless learned that people do see their leisure, in general, as intrinsically rewarding, as relatively uncoerced activity they initiate for their own fulfillment.

Today, we know considerably more about this link between leisure fulfillment (discussed in the earlier literature as "satisfaction") and the motivational components of particular leisure activities. Mannell and Kleiber (1997, pp. 208-209) provide a review of some of the research in this area, most of which, however, centers on casual leisure. Be that as it may, serious leisure research can also make a significant contribution here, founded as much of it has been on the use of qualitative methods in direct exploration of particular amateur, hobbyist, and volunteer activities. Using this approach has led to discovery of a distinctive set of rewards for each activity examined (Stebbins, 1992, 1996a, 1998a; Arai & Pedlar, 1997). In these studies the participant's leisure fulfillment has been found to stem from a constellation of special rewards gained from the activity, whether it is playing baseball, singing barbershop songs, or serving as president of a theatre society. Furthermore, these rewards are not only satisfying in themselves, but also satisfying as counterweights to various costs encountered in the activity.

It is surprising, perhaps, but every serious leisure activity does have its costs as well – a distinctive combination of tensions, dislikes, and disappointments – which each participant confronts in individualistic fashion. The many epics experienced while pursing the three hobbies considered in this book, some of which were described in the preceding chapter, exemplify well certain costs that can emerge with participation in them. But epics notwithstanding these hobbyists still regard their activity as enormously fulfilling – as (serious) leisure – because it also offers a variety of powerful rewards. Put more precisely, then, the drive to gain deep fulfillment in serious leisure is the drive to experience the rewards of a given leisure activity, such that its costs are seen by the participant as more or less insignificant in comparison. Likewise, the careers considered in the preceding chapter derive their motivational property from continuous, long-term pursuit of these rewards, notwithstanding partially offsetting costs.

To facilitate their discussion in this chapter, the ten rewards set out in Chapter 2 are listed below in short form (See page 36 for complete list.). They are the everyday life components of leisure motivation that have heretofore been largely assumed.

1. Personal enrichment
2. Self-fulfillment
3. Self-expression
4. Self-image
5. Self-gratification
6. Recreation
7. Financial return

8. Social attraction
9. Group accomplishment
10. Contribution to maintain and develop the group

In my different studies of amateurs, hobbyists, and volunteers, the interviewees, depending on the activity, often gave different weightings to these rewards so as to reflect their importance relative to each other. Moreover, these studies revealed some notable variations among small numbers of individual participants in the same activity. For instance, financial return has been by far the weakest reward in serious leisure for, among the few amateurs and volunteers who have been paid, the remuneration has been too small to contribute significantly to their livelihood. Nevertheless, some common ground exists, for the studies show that, in terms of their personal importance, most serious leisure participants rank self-enrichment and self-gratification as number one and number two, although to find either reward, the participant must have sufficient levels of relevant skill, knowledge, and experience. In other words, self-fulfillment, which was often ranked third in importance, is also highly rewarding in serious leisure.

I followed the same procedure in the present study, which was to ask each interviewee first to examine a list of the aforementioned rewards (printed on a file card) and then to rank them from highest to lowest in terms of personal importance, giving no rank whatsoever to those that failed to apply. After discussing in detail the rewards and their ranking with each respondent, I encouraged this person, in line with the exploratory mission of the study, to add other rewards to the list, if they could think of any. Over the years of research on serious leisure, this is how the list grew and some of the rewards came to be more precisely conceptualized. To determine the ranks for an entire sample, weights were first assigned to the ranked rewards of each respondent and, to construct a collective profile, the weighted ranks were then summed up for each reward for the subsample in question.

Recently, several scholars have joined me in arguing that serious leisure experiences also have a negative side that must not be overlooked (Codina, 1999; Harries & Currie, 1998; Siegenthaler & Gonsalez, 1997; Lee, Dattilo, & Howard, 1994). In line with this reasoning, I have always asked my respondents to discuss the costs they face in their serious leisure. But so far, it has been impossible to develop a general list of them, as has been done for rewards, since the costs tend to be highly specific to each serious leisure activity. Thus each activity studied to date has been found to have its own constellation of costs, but as the respondents see them, they are invariably and heavily outweighed in importance by the rewards of the activity.

Rewards

The weightings of the rewards felt by all three groups of hobbyists turned out to be very much the same across the overall sample and very much like those assigned by other serious leisure groups that have been examined from this angle. Here, too, personal enrichment, self-fulfillment, and self-gratification are the three most prominent rewards, along with rather less frequent mention of self-expression. Self-image and social attraction, compared with these three, were seen as still weaker, with the rest not even being cited by most respondents. Neither sex of respondent nor level of his or her experience was reflected in the weighting of the rewards.

Since these rewards are found at the very core of the person's motivation for steady, serious participation in climbing, kayaking, and snowboarding, it is important to hear directly from some of the participants about their feelings toward these rewards. In this regard a male climber said of the personally enriching aspects of his hobby:

> One of my values in life is to experience as many things as possible, and climbing is kind of considered one thing. But you get a lot of emotions and also it takes you physically a lot of places you haven't been before and it continues to do that for me. I like that, all the different emotions

I feel — as you push yourself harder you are always pushing your body harder as well. That is somewhat a cherished experience, just those moments. And also with my climbing it is not necessarily that I am always trying to do something like the hardest thing around. I often just want to see different areas, to see as many different places so I think maybe at the time that one isn't the top with me but in the future I think it will be. And eventually as you get older you start declining, and your performance is . . . I won't be climbing as hard when I'm fifty, so I will always have these, have experiences at no matter what level.

Another male climber discussed the reward of self-fulfillment:

Self-fulfillment . . . is important to me. The whole reason why I do it is because it is important to me. If it wasn't then possibly you could be doing it for somebody else and that is not what it is about. It is not selfish because it is something that you love and that comes from deep within me. It's something that I don't want to ever lose, because it gives me such great insight into life. Developing my skills and my abilities and my knowledge and the fulfillment. I get these because I have understood it, I have gotten myself there, and you know, I have found that my abilities progress, they get better . . . And as I understand more and work harder and as I do other things, I find that more things open up to me and I do end up getting more enjoyment out of it I suppose. But that would be for you. . . . I think if you are climbing or doing any of this for anybody else then you are doing it for the wrong reason.

A third male described well the reward of self-gratification in mountain climbing:

Well self-gratification, if that means pure pleasure of the moment, is what I search for the most, and that is why my climbing is usually that kind of climbing where you can go climbing everyday. There is not much preparation, not much planning, not too much travelling, because what I like to do is climb itself more than the process [of getting to it]. That is why I don't go on mountaineering trips. There are too many things that come in the way of just the pure moment, the pure fun of climbing, so I guess that is pretty important.

The kayakers also ranked highly the three rewards of self-enrichment, self-fulfillment, and self-gratification, but in addition, those of recreation and social attraction. I suspect that it is the strong sense of flow that so quickly emerges when roaring through wild water passages, that explains the feeling of getting regenerated from this experience. Flow would be this strong in mountain climbing only at "cruxes" (places of exceptional risk and exposure), a hobby where, in harmony with this observation, recreation was noticeably less often listed as a reward. As for social attraction, kayakers commonly boat together in groups and may camp out a night or two during a trip with the same gang. The shop talk, bonding, camaraderie, and building of trust around a common natural challenge combine to generate an appealing social life for kayakers, which is unparalleled in the other two hobbies.

A male kayaker describes the social attraction that his hobby holds for him:

> One of the key things is the social attraction, in that normally people that I kayak with I really enjoy spending time with. And we can spend time doing something that all of us have a common interest or love for and have spent enough time to get to the level or ability that we are at. But at the same time I would enjoy paddling with somebody that was new to the sport just as much as paddling with someone who is very experienced. [This is] because I like to share the experiences I have had [in order] to interest somebody or show them how incredibly fun or how many rewards you can get from just picking kayaking. People that I have met over the last fifteen years in kayaking have just been fabulous.

A female kayaker explains how her hobby helps regenerate her after life's routine demands:

> And I chose the recreation/regeneration, because in a lot of ways, it is a stress relief. Not that I have a terribly stressful life, but it sure is nice to just up and go paddling a river, to be away from the city, to be away from the thought of work, to get absorbed in something completely different and something that is fun and challenging and exhilarating. And that's a nice switch from the day-to-day work life for sure. And a needed one; I would go crazy if I couldn't do that. That is why I hated Calgary, because I was stuck.

The snowboarders reported close to the same pattern of rewards as the mountain climbers; self-enrichment, self-fulfillment, and self-gratification were the most prominent, with self-image mentioned least. The boarders, however, were roughly evenly divided on the reward of social attraction. A slight majority held it to be a reward of little significance.

Turning first to fulfillment, a male snowboarder described just how self-actualizing his hobby can be:

> Self-fulfillment for sure. I love, like, just honing my skills as a snowboarder; always want to learn new tricks. Like you might see something on a video, and you will, like, rewind it and watch it over, play it in "slo mo," and just figure out how he is doing the trick. And then it looks super hard. Then you are standing on the jump, and this is going through your head ten or twenty times over and over and then just try to do it. Especially the first try it is the neatest feeling. Sometimes it is frustrating, because you will just have an off-day so you won't . . . even an off-day those are still fun.

And what is gratifying about snowboarding? A female boarder explains:

> I listed self-gratification, because of the pure pleasure. It is just something that I like to do. It is what I decide to do so; it is my achievement that is how I see it. That is how I spend my free time, and I also think it is a good workout. It is a nice way to go out for some fresh air and hang out with your friends. And, you know, it is a good excuse for exercise, a fun way to do exercise. That is why I do it. It is my sport during the winter.

Disappointments

The disappointments found in these hobbies indirectly tell us something about the high points available in them. That is, a disappointment here is often an experience that denies the participant an anticipated thrill, or at the very least, an attractive session of routine self-fulfillment.

The climbers talked about three types of disappointment. The most common was getting injured, such that, for an extended period of time, the person was unable to participate in the activity at a fulfilling level. Sometimes a broken bone is the basis for disappointment. One male climber "blew out" his knee.

But I guess – a friend of mine tackled me just for being stupid, we were going to do an ice climb and we were just about there and you know just being silly and being funny – I blew out my knee and I lost the rest of the ice climbing season last year. It wasn't much, but I had things left that I wanted to do, and I had to sit on my bum for quite a long time in a full hip to ankle brace. And the fact that they [his climbing friends] went and climbed one that I had my eye on all season, that really bums me out. Injuries really get me down. Like it doesn't really work for me at all; can't really sit around and watch people do stuff.

Climbers can also be disappointed in themselves (as suggested in this chapter's epigraph) in, for example, not pushing on when tired or continuing along the route when frightened by a section. Third, disappointment sometimes springs from weak climbers in the climbing party, who seriously slow down, if not limit, its progress up the mountain. A variant of this disappointment is having an outing ruined by an unpleasant personality in the group, a situation that underscores the importance of the social side of this hobby. Most people climb with others with whom, for the day, they form a team, and if the trip is to be enjoyable, those others have to be easy to get on with.

Disappointment in self, was, among the kayakers, by far the most common sentiment of this genre. And most frequently noted in this category was having to swim, signifying personal failure at mastering the Eskimo roll.

I used to swim a lot and have to get rescued. I didn't like that; that was disappointing. And it would put more pressure on me, and it would kind of ruin my day if I had to swim, even if the rest of the day went really good the swim was the stopper. You could have the best day of kayaking in your life, but if you have a swim in there, then it wasted your day. And nothing nasty, it didn't scare me to swim it just disappointed me that I couldn't pull a roll off, and that's why I have really worked on that for rodeo and for play. It is the most basic move, and you will get your first roll the first day that you are out. But its doing that roll consistently under pressure and in bigger water or in a rapid section, so what I have found is that I have abandoned one side. I still have that roll when I need it, but nine times out of ten I will roll on the left side because I am comfortable with it. — *male kayaker*

A few of the kayaking interviewees also mentioned disappointment in having an off-day, during which their usual skills were not up to par. Injuries that sideline the hobbyist and failure to perform well in a competition were the next two most common disappointments. Of note is that a minority of these respondents said they could remember no disappointments in this hobby.

Injuries and poor snow conditions topped the list of disappointments among the snowboarders. Meager accumulations of snow have, in recent years, plagued them as well as skiers, both alpine and cross-country. Warm weather has worsened this problem by creating icy conditions, which are a main cause of serious accidents. Disappointments with self, though less frequently cited than with the first two, did nonetheless occur. In general this was a matter of failure in skills normally available to the individual or failure to have developed the skills required for the terrain at hand or for a particular snowboard park manoeuvre. The result: the rider falls or gets injured, sometimes both.

Tensions

The principal tension in this sample of climbers comes from competition among members of the climbing party, a relationship (held by several of those with experience elsewhere) to be especially characteristic of the Bow Valley mountaineering scene. Sometimes competition manifested itself in a wrangle over who was going to lead a multi-pitch ascent or, on rarer occasion, in a rush to see who would be first to reach the summit. One woman, – she was far from alone among female climbers in this regard – felt this tension when with her boyfriend, who she said always wanted to dominate the climb (this was the only area in the three types of cost on which male and female respondents varied). Another climber opined that competition often emerged among those seeking commercial equipment sponsorships. Contests of this sort are more likely to occur in the Canmore area, however, with its large contingent of first-rate alpinists, than in most other climbing communities.

Tension can also arise over technical issues. For instance, something can unexpectedly go wrong during a climb, like a bolt pulling loose or someone getting serious injured by falling rock. Additionally, tensions may mount in the climbing party when one of them tries to climb in a way considered too risky by the rest, because they see such behavior as beyond that person's ability (and perhaps their own). This tension works both ways, however, for the climber in question usually views the others as weaker climbers, who are spoiling the fun. Furthermore, such uncertainties as the weather and lack of familiarity with the route may lead to tests of technical ability for all concerned, raising the level of tension in the process.

Tensions in the world of kayaking come from, among other sources, paddling with others who you do not know. Experiencing this widely mentioned sentiment can be avoided by always going with the same group, in fact a common practice in this hobby. Nonetheless, some kayakers some of the time, because they are new to the area or have no trans-portation, for instance, find themselves in unfamiliar company. Under these conditions they worry about such issues as the abilities of their new found colleagues (especially to lead), their attention to safety considerations, and the possibility that the trip could be spoiled by an accident requiring rescue, a loss of or damage to a boat, a long hike through the woods, and the like. In the words of a male kayaker with a great deal of experience:

> Once somebody said that they were bringing somebody along to run Toby Creek with us, and I said well I wasn't really interested in going if that person was going. I knew the person. I sort of briefly met them [person and friends], but I knew that they were not up to that caliber of paddling. When I go paddle rivers like that that are fairly difficult, I don't

really want people there who are going to be a liability, and that is for
their safety as well as my own safety if they get into a position or I am
put into a position of having to help rescue somebody. Again, I have
nothing against taking people down rivers who are not at that level, but
if they are obviously not up to it then I am not really interested.

Paddling unknown creeks and rivers can also be tense, even
if there is also a dash of thrill in this new experience. Even
known watercourses can hold surprises like recently downed
trees and, in the Rockies, wide fluctuations in water levels. Both
tensions rest on estimations by individual kayakers of their own
abilities *vis-à-vis* the water conditions at the time. Further, a
premium is placed on these abilities by the fact that, unlike
skiing and cycling, for instance, where participants can stop and
assess terrain before negotiating it, kayakers must often decide
what to do while on the move. And move they do, for the
kayak, to be maneuverable, must be propelled along the surface
of the creek or river at a rate faster than that of the current at
that level. Nonetheless, kayakers do sometimes find the equiv-
alent of a stopping place – e.g., an eddy – from which to assess
upcoming challenges.

Two additional, though less common, tensions in kayaking
were also discussed. Thus some women, like their mountain
climbing counterparts, described a special tension they experienced when with a male friend with whom they routinely
paddled: pressure to try to do something for which they lacked
confidence. They were, however, made to feel they should be
able to do this. It can also be tense for some kayakers when
certain members of their boating party try to outdo each other,
leading those members into situations that require skills they do
not have.

Snowboarding was often described by the respondents as an
activity free of tension. The main tension, mentioned by a
majority of them, revolved around the snowboard parks. Boarders
get angry with skiers who occasionally wander into this, the

exclusive domain of the former, as well as with other boarders, almost always novices, who do not know how to use the parks.

> I think one of the major tensions would be between the ski and the snowboard school – especially the skiers that have been around for a long time. They just haven't really accepted snowboarding and that it is here to stay – they are kind of like, yeah, a couple of years whatever, just another fad. Other than that, not really a whole lot of tension snowboarding. – *female snowboarder*

There is, as well, some tension with skiers on slopes outside the parks, particularly on days when the slopes are crowded. Moreover, it turns out, such conflict is also found outside the Canmore-Banff corridor. Vaske and colleagues (2000) observed it in five ski resorts in Colorado, with both skiers and snowboarders complaining in the researchers' survey about the behavior of each other.

Dislikes

Dislikes are not generally a problem in these three hobbies, which should not be surprising, since the presence of numerous dislikes would become sufficient grounds for abandoning the activity for something more agreeable. Nearly all respondents could note but one dislike, and most of these were idiosyncratic. For the climbers the only shared dislike (shared by about half the sample) centered on the attitude of some climbers. "Air of superiority" seems to describe best this orientation. Some climbers, obviously to the displeasure of other climbers, think they are special compared with other outdoor people, and appear to want to use every occasion to tell all who are present why it is they stand out so. This is typically done by vaingloriously inventorying their climbing exploits and recounting in detail the great many challenges they have met, as a sort of personal operationalization of Bourdieu's stratificational concept of distinction mentioned in Chapter 1. A male climber described this dislike:

> Where people are very full of themselves, and they will sit there and tell you what they climbed and when they climbed it. You know you are

talking about something and, you know, and it is like this climb is so beautiful. Or you have just been out climbing, and it is, oh, where did you climb and you told them and they say like, oh, did you really do that? It is like, it seems a little pretentious – not the reason why we are out there.

A substantial minority of the kayakers had no dislikes of any kind. Among those who had even one, and one was almost without exception the limit, congested rivers and rodeo sites were the most frequently mentioned (by four respondents). For instance, on a crowded day a paddler might have to wait 20 minutes or more before gaining access to a popular standing wave. Additionally, three respondents disliked the kayaker's version of the air of superiority that annoys some mountain climbers. Moreover, its ingredients are similar: annoying recitations of exploits accomplished and challenges met, all served up in an aura of "I am better than you."

Conclusions

Returning to the history of research on leisure motivation set out at the beginning of this chapter, I have presented in detail in the course of it several everyday life components of the motivation of individual climbers, kayakers, and snowboarders. These components – the rewards of the hobbies – number among the "meaningful and appropriate factors" affecting leisure fulfillment for these hobbyists, factors that were missing in the older explanations of motivation. These are the details of their leisure motivation, which when joined with their many experiences of flow and a sense of their own leisure careers (as discussed in Chapters 1, 2, and 4), offer a much more complete picture of the intense appeal of these activities than provided by earlier models.

Not only were earlier models short on everyday life details of leisure motivation, they were also (even more seriously) short of details on the costs that participants must deal with, even if they nevertheless minimize their effect. Although not all costs can be considered in this light, there is certainly substantial motivation in the propensity, especially prominent in these hobbies, to try to conquer adversity, adversity being seen as cost. Thus, it is unpleasant at the time to be freezing in subzero temperatures on a snowboard slope or suffering with tired muscles on the last pitch of a multi-pitch climb. Some kayakers, used to the warmer rivers of central and eastern Canada, complained about the ice cold water that runs in Alberta's mountain streams. But once these difficult moments are mastered and the challenge of nature is met despite them, the participant is ready to bask in the heady feeling of accomplishment. This is one of many unique motivational features of serious leisure.

Given the profound attractiveness of these rewards, it is no wonder that the hobbyists of this study try, in diverse ways and with varying degrees of success, to arrange their lives such that they can experience the rewards with the greatest frequency and intensity possible. And, in this respect, there is, to repeat, little difference between the sexes or between those hobbyists with great experience and those with little experience in the hobby. Meanwhile, the motivation to pursue a serious leisure activity has consequences that are felt well beyond the activity itself. The nearly universal wish for more time and money to better and more frequently engage in the hobby affects relations at home, at work, and in the community. It may also influence the person's socioeconomic standing.

Chapter 6

Lifestyles and Social Worlds

The love of money as a possession – as distinguished from the love of money as a means to the enjoyments and realities of life – will be recognized for what it is, a somewhat disgusting morbidity, one of those semi-criminal, semi-pathological propensities which one hands over with a shudder to the specialists in mental disease

John Maynard Keynes
Essays in Persuasion [1931, pt. V]

In this study, lifestyle was examined along three dimensions. Concerning the activity dimension, I inquired about amount of time spent doing the central activity, number of memberships in related organizations, and proportion of close friends and relatives participating in it. This gave insight into the social worlds of the three hobbies. Additionally, I asked about acceptance of the hobby and involvement in it by spouses, partners, boyfriends, and girlfriends, a query that also included, where appropriate, other members of the respondent's immediate family. This is referred to here summarily, and as a convenience, simply as the family dimension. Finally, along the work dimension, lifestyle was studied according to the way the activity relates to the participant's employment, conflicts with it (if they occurred at all), and in the eyes of the respondent, blends or clashes with the job.

Lifestyle and social world – two important mesostructural concepts in this study – are in many ways closely related. For this reason, both are covered in this chapter, where we will look at the four types of members of social world as found in the three hobbies. We start, however, with lifestyle and its activity dimension.

Activity Dimension

The climbers are a busy group, in good part because they can be active much of the year. At time of interviewing they averaged 143 days of climbing (ice and rock) per year, with one maintaining that he climbed four days a week (208 days a year). This heavy involvement in their hobby did not include participating in related organizations, since only one in the sample said he was a member of one. Moreover, the friendships of these climbers revolve substantially around the activity; an average of 80 percent of close friends and relatives were also serious climbers. Nor were these circles of like-minded enthusiasts especially homogeneous in terms of age, for their ages often ranged across 20 years, with the typical respondent falling somewhere in the middle.

What counts in climbing is that participants in the climbing party of the day be willing and able to tackle the same levels of difficulty. As long as this condition is met, age, and for that matter sex of participant, are of little or no concern. By contrast, level of experience is a foremost consideration.

Kayaking is pursued in the Alberta Rockies mainly from April into October, with beginnings and ends of seasons varying according to water levels and air temperatures. During the season this sample was extremely active, averaging 72 days a season, with the range running from 24 days to over 150. Furthermore, these kayakers are more organized than the climbers, for nearly half the sample belonged to a kayaking club or association and many, though presently not members, had before moving to Canmore, been members in another locality.

As for close friends in the hobby, the average was 55 percent of all friends, with three interviewees saying they had few friends there and three others saying between 80 and 100 percent of their friends were kayakers. The sample was roughly split as to the age range of these friends. The large minority had friends more or less the same age, while a small majority said their kayaking friends' ages spanned 20 years or more, even including a few sturdy souls in their sixties. Friends tended to be of both sexes, but were usually of the same level of experience as the respondent.

Given the comparative shortness of the snowboarding season, which in the Canmore-Banff area, seldom lasts longer than six months, the snowboarders, at an average of 88 days per year, can be qualified as more active than the kayakers and possibly even more so than the climbers. Many of the latter can and do climb (rock or ice) nearly all the year. As with the kayakers about half the snowboarders belonged to an organization, usually the Alberta Snowboard Association (an entity entitling members to participate in the races it sponsors).

Of the three hobbyist groups, the snowboarders had the greatest tendency to limit their friendships to their own kind; on average 91 percent of friends were other snowboarders, within a range of 55 to 100 percent. Six respondents said all their friends were in the same hobby. For half the sample these friends were close in age, while the other half had many snowboarding friends substantially younger and older than they. As with the other two hobbies, both males and females counted as friends, but they tended to be homogenous according to skill and experience.

Family Dimension

All respondents with a spouse or steady partner were asked if this person accepted, rejected, or tolerated the hobbyist activity of the former. Among the climbers who had a boyfriend or girlfriend (none was married or had a partner), all said that this person accepted their climbing passion. Indeed, all the boyfriends and girlfriends were themselves climbers. Still, acceptance did not always prevent occasional friction from bubbling up around climbing-related issues, even if those issues were unlikely to be centered on such relational matters as spending too much time at or money on the hobby. For example, one female respondent recounted a disagreement with her boyfriend over whether to go on a particular climb.

> We were planning on going up Robson this weekend coming up, and Tim [pseudonym] was coming along. I heard he had been talking to some climbers that he knows, and we had heard that the conditions were really bad on it. There are very few summits; it had two feet of snow, etc., etc. When we first started talking about it I was really excited, but I was planning to train a little beforehand to get ready. But I haven't for whatever reason. I haven't had the time to get in the shape I would like to be to climb it. So I sort of said yesterday I am not sure I am really ready for it, especially looking at the conditions. And I was under the impression that it was Paul [pseudonym of boyfriend] and my trip that we were planning, but I didn't realize that Tim and Paul had been planning it for two years. I had sort of been hinting well maybe we could do something else, but Paul was adamant, no I am doing Robson and that is it. So we had a little bit of an argument about that, 'cause he was not being very flexible. I was admitting my weaknesses and I didn't feel ready for it, and I was basically getting ditched, because I wasn't ready and Paul and Tim were going to go anyway.

With five exceptions, two who only tolerated their spouse's hobby and three others who rejected it, the kayaking sample reported enthusiastic acceptance of this form of leisure, whether by a spouse, girlfriend/boyfriend, or unmarried partner. Such an attitude comes as no surprise, for like the mountain climbers, all but one of those who were accepting were themselves kayakers. Those who tolerated the hobby were married, while those who rejected it were partners.

> I've lost girlfriends in the past because of my kayaking. Right now Alice [pseudonym] accepts it, because it is a new relationship. She wanted me to go visit her parents last weekend, and I almost missed paddling. She tried to suck me in. [Still,] I have changed quite a bit, because now I know it is important to be with the person. On shitty weekends we hang out and find hot-tubs. . . . I've lost girlfriends, because I'm never home with paddling trips. — *male kayaker*

Halfway between accepts and tolerates. She knows how much I like to kayak, but she has to tolerate it because it means I'm not walking the dog or free to do something with her. . . . Not sharing. It creates tension when really I have an urge and a need to go. Know I can't always paddle. It wouldn't be right. I made a commitment to her. . . . She doesn't paddle. She did try it a bit with rafting work, and she can roll up to class-three water. The cold water out here is an issue [compared with back east]. What would we do with the dog? She has a reborn fear of being trapped in a boat, because it has been a while since she was out.
— *male kayaker*

Approximately a quarter of the kayaking sample had no steady relationship with someone of the opposite sex, while 10 (5 males, 5 females), or 42 percent, were married. Thus the kayakers, compared with the climbing sample, presented a markedly different pattern of familial relationships. These discrepancies, if not simply an artifact of the sampling procedure, are difficult to explain using the data gathered in this study. Furthermore, those in steady relationships do not always link up with a man or woman of the same level of skill and experience as the respondent. This discrepancy can, in itself, be a source of friction between the couple, as some of the preceding quotations from both kayakers and climbers demonstrate.

All in the snowboard sample reported that their boyfriends or girlfriends accepted their hobby. The sample contained only one married participant, though only three of its members said they had no steady relationship with someone of the opposite sex. In harmony with the pattern found in the other two groups, nearly all boyfriends and girlfriends of members of the sample were also snowboarders. A female snowboarder talked about her earlier relationship with a man who could no longer participate in the hobby.

R: He was a snowboarder, and then he had a knee injury and he didn't snowboard after that. So he became a sledder. And it was really conflicting, because he would sled and I would snowboard. Or if you know it was his day off, I would be that greedy that I would go out snowboarding. I wouldn't stay home and hang out with him just because I am not . . .

don't want to sit around the house and watch T.V. all day. . . . Yeah, so that really conflicted a lot. He liked it when I went out and snowboarded, but it is not something that we did together at all.

I: *So did that cause the break up?*

R: It was pretty much like he went to Ontario and I stayed here. I snowboard. Like I said I am kind of greedy about it, you know. Like on his days off he would want me to stay and hang out, and I'd be, like, no I'll see you when I get home from the slopes.

Toward the opposite end of the spectrum, consider the appreciation of this male of his wife's ability on snowboard.

She used to be a snowboarding instructor. She has been riding for six years and really likes it, but she is not as passionate as me. She rode more before she had our daughter. She is much slower than me. I'm way beyond her but she is good. It is awesome to see people excel. Sometimes I have to say to her, you're not ready, you can't come. If it is a hairy situation and she might break down and peak out, she ups the limit. She only jumps eight feet.

Work Dimension

The climbers all had some post-secondary education, ranging from training at a technical college to four-year university degrees, with most of the sample having completed between two and four years of university work. They have not, however, been inclined to find office jobs based on this educational background. Rather, they have sought work with wildlife or other employment out of doors, including for some, mountain guiding. One was employed as a paramedic and firefighter, another in retail sales, while a third performed odd jobs.

For much of the sample work was little more than a way to make a living. That is, when asked by the interviewer about which was more important for personal identity, fulfillment, and excitement, all but one said it was climbing and not the job they held at the time.

I work to make money and earn a living. I just happen to do something that I really love and make good money at cause I run my own company. So I get a lot of satisfaction from my business, but you couldn't even compare it to the satisfaction that I get from climbing. It is like, if I was in love with someone now, I would say you can't compare the enrichment and fulfillment I get from being intimate with someone with my career or even define it.

There was a feeling among the majority of climbers that work too often gets in the way of their hobby. If nothing else, work was seen to take up time, some of which could otherwise be used to climb. Worse, perhaps, was that most felt work fatigues them, leaving them in less than optimal condition for pursuing their hobby. This was an understandable lament, given that most work out of doors, where they are frequently on the move. Climbing also fatigues most respondents for work, but that condition bothers them much less than the reverse.

Kayakers

The kayakers were the most educated of the three hobbyist groups. Three-quarters of them had earned four-year university degrees, including two people who had some graduate training to their credit. Consequently, the kayakers, compared with the other two subsamples, were exceptionally represented in managerial, semiprofessional, and professional positions.

Having high-level, responsible work does not, however, necessarily translate into conflict between work and serious leisure. Indeed, the kayaker sample was roughly divided on this question. For some of them having flexible work hours helps greatly to obviate such tension, or, in kayaking, having work such as school teaching that leaves summers free. But, for those for whom work did conflict with leisure, time was typically the issue: time working could have been used to kayak. Furthermore, close to 50 percent of the sample said work left them tired for kayaking, whereas a solid majority said their hobby left them fatigued the next day for their employment. Still, this was a "happy" physical state, it having resulted from doing what one loves.

If tension between work and leisure could sometimes be avoided, it was much less often possible for the large number of kayakers to avoid the fact that the latter is far more appealing than the former. Here, too, it is a question of the hobby being more exciting than the job. A male kayaker, who works in a saw mill, put it this way:

> Yeah, work is kind of dull even though . . . even if you are running equipment and there is no radio or anything like that to make the time pass. So what I have done at one of my jobs is put up a lot of kayak posters all over the mill. So whatever job I am at, usually there is a kayaking poster there. And I can reflect back on what I did this week or what I did last week or who I paddled with or the times we had. And that makes time pass.

Notwithstanding the high-level of work engaged in by most of the kayaking sample, the vast majority, when it comes to fulfillment, identity, and excitement, would choose their hobby over their employment. The comments of the respondents, in this regard, are most revealing.

> R: I guess right now that there is no doubt in my mind that I love my leisure activities, and I don't love my job. I don't hate my job, so right now my leisure activities are a more pure form of enjoyment and satisfaction. Would I be happy if all I did was my leisure activities? No — I have to have other things to do as well. Certainly I do envision life not being an X [professional occupation]; there are lots of other things I could do. [But] I have absolutely no desire to give up kayaking or any of my other leisure. I will never give kayaking up I don't think, but I may give up X.
>
> I: *Which do you identify with more, your work role or your leisure role?*
>
> R: I think my leisure role. — *female kayaker*

> R: I would choose kayaking, but I like the money from work. I don't like living like a bum on fifteen thousand [dollars] for ten years. It's a sacrifice for now. . . . Things are better now. . . . I've been poor in the past, and lived in a trailer. — *male kayaker*

R: Work to play, kayaker for sure – would spend most of my time talking about kayaking. It is of course situation specific. In engineering, it is
totally boring. At the moment I am very negative about my work. This is
the most unconscious period of work in my life. Now I take lots of
"sickies" [sick days], and do the bare minimum required to not receive
warnings. Have to wear lots of sunscreen to hide my days out in leisure.
– *male kayaker*

Yet, approximately 20 percent of the sample, when it came
to fulfillment and identity, and excitement, was unable to make
the hypothetical choice between their work and their serious
leisure. They liked both, and some saw a balance involving
these two that significantly enhanced their personal well-being.

There are different forms of satisfaction. I get the satisfaction from
making myself feel good, especially through leisure, especially when
pushing one's limits. Work satisfaction is more through achievement for
getting the job done and recognition for a good job, but it doesn't give
me a feeling of well-being that I get through leisure activities. – *male
kayaker*

A female kayaker observed, "I can't give up one for the other. I
struggle with this. A career and learning is important. That's
why I couldn't just go on the rodeo circuit. I'm trying to find a
way to make both work, because both play a big role [in my
life]." This minority was fortunate enough to have found work
that, in intensity of appeal and fulfillment, matched their
leisure, work I have referred to elsewhere as "devotee work"
(Stebbins, 2004b).

For the majority of kayakers, however, it was their kayaking,
and sometimes other serious leisure pursuits like cycling and
skiing, that constituted their central life interests (Dubihn,
1992). For this group work mattered primarily because it
provided the means to pursue these interests, a sort of necessary
evil. In all this level of skill and experience as well as sex of
respondent mattered little; the subsample was not differentiated
along these lines.

Snowboarders

The snowboarders had the lowest level of educational attainment of the three groups, which partly reflects their much younger average age (over six years separated them from the other two). Approximately half the sample had received a grade 12 education, the other half had completed a year or two of, in most instances, university work. Their lines of employment reflected these qualifications: cook, janitor, laborer, store clerk, restaurant server, manager of a small store. A couple of respondents worked winters as snowboard instructors.

Work still conflicted often or occasionally with the hobby for the majority of this group, with those employed in the snowboarding industry (e.g., instructing, maintaining a snow park) finding the greatest harmony between their work and leisure. Moreover, most of the sample said, with regret, that their work wore them out, leaving them in less than optimal form for riding the slopes. A female snowboarder gave an example.

> I have been working the last three nights and [that] coincided with the last two days of competition. So working until three in the morning, up at seven and doing the competition all day — I could have definitely done better if I wasn't working the night before. That was an unfortunate thing, in a way, when it conflicted.

All but two of this group also noted that snowboarding tired them out for work, although here too, this was anything but a lamentable state. And like the other two groups the hobby of this one was much on the mind during work hours. Indeed, only one snowboarder said he did not think much about his hobby while on the job.

The snowboarders, as a group, were clearest about the place of their hobby in their lives *vis-à-vis* the place there of their present employment. All but one said snowboarding was where they could find the greatest fulfillment, identity, and excitement. The sole exception to this generalization was a snowboard instructor. Responses to this probe were commonly spontaneous, strong, and unequivocal; literally no one said that, because their work was also immensely attractive, they were unable to make such a choice.

> I can really get into things. And when I do find something that I want to do and I am prepared to continue my education to achieve my goal, there is no telling what is going to happen. I am sure that snowboarding is still going to be on the stove. It may hit a back burner for a little bit or for a season or something, but depending on – I don't know what I want to do so who knows – I might find something that takes me to a place where I can't snowboard. And if the time comes then I will have to make the decision, but in the foreseeable future and without furthering my education, there is nothing that would keep me from snowboarding and biking. *– male snowboarder*
>
> **I:** *If you had to choose between the work that you have, and it can be either or both jobs, and the leisure that you participate in, which can be climbing or snowboarding, as the pursuit that gives you the most satisfaction which, if either, would you choose?*
>
> **R:** My sports.
>
> **I:** *Why is that?*
>
> **R:** Right now, because this [work] isn't the field that I want to be in for the rest of my life, so I am mostly out here for my sports not my work. I like my work, but it is just a way to be able to do all the leisure stuff. . . . It is kind of just a way to pay the bills. *– female snowboarder*

As with the other two hobbies, sex of respondent and level of skill and experience were not correlated with these views on the comparative importance of work and serious leisure.

Social Worlds

The concept of social world was defined and briefly described in Chapter 2, where it was presented as a main component of the unique ethos that helps differentiate serious leisure from its counterpart, casual leisure. But to understand fully its mesostructural and motivational properties, the idea must now be spelled out in greater detail than was done earlier. Accordingly, every social world contains four types of members, identified by Unruh (1979; 1980) as "strangers," "tourists," "regulars," and "insiders." *Strangers* are intermediaries who normally participate little in the leisure activity itself, but who nonetheless do something important to make it possible or to enhance it. The people who maintain snowboard parks, sell and repair equipment, and publish and sell relevant books and magazines are among the strangers in mountaineering, kayaking, and snowboarding. Given the popularity of after-hours post-mortems of hobbyist outings on mountain faces, slopes, and rivers, and the general lure of shop talk at any time, people who own and run the bars, restaurants, and coffee shops frequented by hobbyists who gravitate there for this purpose can also be classified as strangers.

Tourists are temporary participants in a social world; they have come on the scene momentarily for entertainment, diversion, or profit. Most amateur and hobbyist activities have publics of some kind, who according to this scheme, can be classified as tourists. The tourist component of the three social worlds under consideration here – i.e., the public that, as spectators, observes one or more of the three hobbyist groups in action – is for the most part limited to the few people who gather along a river bank, at the sides of a snowboard park, in a climbing gym, or around a sport climbing site.

Regulars routinely participate in the social world; in this study they are the hobbyists themselves, at least most of them. For there are also *insiders*; the small number of outstanding participants who show exceptional devotion to, and personal development in, the social world they share, to maintaining it, to advancing it, and especially to providing fascinating displays of excellence. Class 5 and 6 mountain climbers and class IV through VI kayakers are the insiders of their social worlds, while in snowboarding, those who routinely ride the double black diamond runs and perform tricks with *éclat* in the snowboard parks can also be thus classified. Professionals, the very few that exist in these sports, must also be considered insiders, as should the devotees, who were discussed in Chapter 2 with reference to participants. The latter, on the other hand, are, in effect, regulars. Finally, note in passing that those who put on airs of superiority are not necessarily of insider quality, though they certainly hope that others will see them in precisely this light.

In all three hobbies, insiders and regulars – mostly within these two categories but sometimes across them – form into small groups and friendship networks that, together, augmenting the mesostructural cohesiveness of the local hobbyist community and its social world. These include the previously discussed climbing and kayaking groups and sets of snowboarding friends, who routinely "head out" together to engage in their hobby. Note, too, that the idea of small group includes the marital, partnership, and friendship dyad.

Missing from Unruh's conceptualization of social world, but important for this study of serious leisure is the proposition that a vibrant subculture is found there as well, one function of which is to interrelate the "diffuse and amorphous constellations." Consequently, it should be pointed out that members recognize as part of their social world a unique set of special norms, values, beliefs, lifestyles, moral principles, performance standards, and similar shared representations. Only by taking these elements into account can we logically speak about, for example, social stratification in social worlds. Unruh treats of stratification when differentiating insiders from regulars, as we have also just done, and as we did earlier in discussing Bourdieu's (1979) process of distinction. When these hobbyists differentiate, or distinguish, devotees and insiders from participants and regulars, we see another manifestation of such distinction in their social worlds.

And there is a special subculture associated with each nature-challenge hobby. Many elements comprise this subculture, including shared beliefs about the vagaries of the weather, the habits of the wild animals (among kayakers and climbers, bears are the most talked about), the peculiarities of the physical environment, the characteristics of the hobbyists themselves, the nature of their equipment, and so on. But most universal of all in these subcultures is the widely shared interest in risk associated with physical danger, which touches each of the aforementioned elements and others not listed here.

Conclusions

The social worlds of these kayakers, snowboarders, and mountain climbers are reasonably evolved, even if still not as evolved as those in some other serious leisure fields, most notably the hugely complex social world of the hobby of barbershop singing (Stebbins, 1996a). Two areas where the social worlds of the three mountain hobbies are comparatively underdeveloped are that of formal organization (strangers) and that of tourist participation. In fact there are organizations to join, but these hobbyists are not generally inclined to join them, the kayakers and snowboarders showing only somewhat more interest in such affiliation than the climbers. And, as already observed, tourist participation is usually thin in these three areas.

This is not, however, to argue that the social worlds of mountain hobbies are inferior, but only different. Note, for instance, that all three hobbies show a high level of development at the informal level of social world; here small groups and social networks of participants are omnipresent. Moreover, there is no theoretical reason to believe that all leisure social worlds will be similar on all dimensions. And perhaps this study contained an unintended sampling bias in favor of selecting norganized hobbyists, a possibility that future research on these social worlds should definitely explore.

Turning to lifestyle, it is abundantly clear from the data that the three hobbies considered in this book are powerfully attractive to their enthusiasts. They are at once veritable passions and central life interests. But for all this, they are not typically the only leisure love in the lives of these men and women. Many members of all three samples also pursue, sometimes with equal if not greater fervor, one or two other serious leisure activities.

Frequently mentioned in this regard were cycling, skiing (downhill, cross-country, back-country), ultimate frisbee, competitive running, and one of the other two hobbies reported on here. Moreover, some snowboarders, when there is no snow, become skate-boarders. The three samples further rounded out their leisure lifestyles with conditioning activities, although these were sometimes defined as obligatory and not especially pleasant (and as such not really leisure). Finally, some had additional serious leisure passions of a less physically active nature, among them stamp collecting, playing a musical instrument, and hunting or fishing. And we shall see in the next chapter that many also enjoy as casual leisure still other indoor and outdoor activities.

The overall sample tended not to turn to career (serious leisure) volunteering, probably because, as with work, it commonly requires a scheduled commitment that can conflict with plans for climbing, kayaking, or snowboarding. Some members of all three subsamples did, however, occasionally engage in project-based volunteering (see Chapter 2), usually something related to their nature-challenge hobby or another serious leisure activity. Examples include volunteering for the Kananaskis River "Chick Fest," an all-female weekend of instruction in kayaking, the annual Banff Mountain Film Festival, and diverse environmental protection and environmental maintenance projects.

In part, these additional serious leisure pursuits are taken on because the hobbies studied here are seasonal (mountain/ice climbers have two seasons) and their enthusiasts are much too active to accept lying around the rest of the year doing only casual leisure. But there were many climbers who also cycled in the summer, kayakers who also ran competitively, and snowboarders who also skied, almost always the downhill variety. As this study shows, then, people often have time for two, sometimes even, three serious leisure activities, even in the same season. We will return to this point in the final chapter on optimal leisure lifestyle.

Chapter 7

Finding an Optimal Leisure Lifestyle

Increased means and increased leisure are the two
civilizers of man.

Benjamin Disraeli
Speech to the Conservatives of Manchester
[3 April 1872]

In at least one respect life is lived in holistic fashion; typically,
unless retired, disabled, or a child, people work, play, and honor
their nonwork obligations of various kinds with some reasonable sense of how these three spheres intersect in their lives.
Moreover, most people appear to want an agreeable balance
between the three, even if finding this balance often proves
difficult. Indeed, in Western society, a significant part of the
dissonance perturbing modern life is the angst that springs
from a stubborn imbalance that has set in among these three.
For instance, these days, many working adults still fret about
spending too much time on the job (Zuzanek, 1996) or having
to honor too many nonwork obligations (e.g., maintaining the
home, taking the children to scheduled activities, caring for
incapacitated relatives). They also fret, the following pages
suggest, about the way they use their free time.

Many people seem to suffer from a spiritual malaise that
their free time, filled exclusively with casual leisure as it is, is only
minimally interesting, marginally exciting, even if not boring,
at least not yet. This was not, however, a problem besetting the
hobbyists interviewed in this study. Much of their free time is
filled with wonderfully and powerfully interesting and fulfilling
things to do. The big question for nearly all of them, they said
– though evidently not one bothering the vast majority of the
population – was how to find the most appealing casual leisure

available and effectively blend it with their serious leisure. For by successfully combining these two kinds of leisure, the individual can come to enjoy an optimal leisure lifestyle.

In addition to their central concern with serious leisure, the interviews inquired directly into the nature, scope, and meaning of casual leisure for each respondent. Since neither concept is known to the general public, it was necessary for the interviewer, before proceeding with this part of the interview, to explain the two forms and how they differ. This "lesson" was, in some instances, inadequate, for some respondents still offered some of their serious leisure pursuits as instances of casual leisure. In the end, however, discussion between interviewee and interviewer about particular activities resulted in onceptual clarification sufficient for valid exploratory inferences about the casual leisure of the first.

Casual Leisure: Climbers

The two of the most common casual leisure activities for the climbers were watching videos or films in a cinema and socializing with friends, as in, for example, having a coffee, going to dinner, going out for drinks, talking on the telephone, or taking in a party. These two were joined by a third equally common activity: reading. This consisted of reading books, magazines, and more rarely, the newspaper, and included material both related and unrelated to climbing and other outdoor pursuits. Surfing the Internet and watching television were by and large scorned, although some spent small amounts of time in e-mail correspondence with friends and relatives. Whereas several interviewees clearly voiced their dislike for the medium, it should be noted that, unless the viewer can afford a cable connection, television reception in the Canadian Rockies is extremely limited. A few people found casual leisure in walking their dog or playing a musical instrument (typically guitar), and three respondents said they had very little casual leisure. For the latter, life consisted of work, serious leisure, and a few nonwork obligations. When calculated for the entire sample for a typical week and excluding the usual amount of climbing and other serious leisure, the climbers averaged 1.75 hours a day in casual leisure.

In short, the meaning of casual leisure for much of this sample can be summed up in the word "relaxation." Relaxation from climbing and any other serious leisure pursued in the same season, as well as from work. During relaxation a person can reflect on many things, among them past and future sessions in the mountains. During relaxation the individual changes to a slower pace than before, "adds variety to life," as one climber put it, or just takes a physical and mental break from climbing. It is also a period of physical rest from both work and serious leisure, where either requires significant expenditure of energy.

> It is really important to me in the sense that I need the mental break. You need mental and physical breaks from climbing, and so I fill it up with the things that reward me the most. I find them very rewarding. I wouldn't want to live without them, but I wouldn't want to have to choose between climbing and them, 'cause it would be too extreme of a lifestyle to just spend all my time climbing and fucking with my gear. — *female climber*

This was, for all three sets of hobbyists, the most common theme in this section of the interviews.

A smaller number of respondents stressed the need to associate with others, especially nonclimbers, which invariably occurred as casual leisure of the socializing variety as described in the opening paragraph of this section.

> No, I think it is important to have casual leisure, because it is important to develop friendships, and you can't really do that when you are doing serious leisure all the time. It is a big thing there because it is important to develop other pursuits and sides of your personality; the [her] artwork comes in there, but then does that lead into serious leisure? It is just good to be able to reflect and slow down. — *female climber*

Another female climber had this to say:

> Yes, because I guess it makes for a more fulfilling life. If I had no social life at all and just climbed, I don't think I would be as happy in the long run. I also like a lot of variety in my life, and that [casual leisure] adds to the variety. But that variety has to be social.

A smaller number of this sample reflected directly on the balance question introduced at the beginning of this chapter. Balance of free time activities was uppermost in their minds, wherein they saw casual leisure, perched as it is on the other side of the fulcrum from serious leisure, as playing a most important role in this process. A male climber observed that,

> It is becoming more and more important just because climbing is becoming less important. It is not less important, but it is just again, like I said, I am looking for that balance, right? I look at some of the best climbers around and, like, people I really admire, and they have a really good balance between keeping a good view of what is going on around them in the world and stuff like that. And they are also able to perform well at their sport. So I want to read more. It is on my mind, but often it is hard to do. Climbing is pretty cool, too. I do what I can, do more in the winter and, like, shoulder season.

This stance, however, contrasted with that of another climber, who in comparing it with his serious leisure, looked on casual leisure as wasted time.

> R: For myself I believe, if possible, I wouldn't allow for any casual. Very often I am climbing the last few days before work and if possible I am back the day after work. If possible I want to at least be doing something.
>
> I: *What about the winter when you ice climb during the day but you can't ice climb at night? Would you climb at night if you could in the winter?*
>
> R: You mean aside from the times when you are stuck up there?
>
> I: *You are basically saying that casual leisure is something you wouldn't choose. It just happens because you can't climb?*
>
> R: Yeah, that is pretty much it.

I: *Is there anything that you get from casual leisure that is different from what you get from serious leisure? Does it offer you anything? Like hanging out with friends, how is that different from climbing?*

R: I am basically just not very good on casual.

I: *That is why you would rather have less of it?*

R: I try to have more climbing so therefore less casual. I'd go out climbing with one person or ten people, before I'd go for coffee with the same people.

I: *What some people have told me is that my casual leisure is when I get to relax and that is what it gives me. Even though they love whatever, walking the dog or having a coffee it is a different experience and they like that too. So I am just trying to figure out if there is something you get from watching a movie or doing whatever that is different and important or is it always just left over stuff after climbing?*

R: It is sort of mandatory to have that rest or short casual time. I don't believe I get much from it really, definitely not the same sense as climbing.

In all this, male and female interviewees responded much the same, and their level of skill and experience was not a factor here either.

Casual Leisure: Kayakers

The most common casual leisure interests among the kayakers were reading books and magazines, socializing and, unlike the climbers, watching television and walking their dog. In this regard, giving substance to the proposition expressed earlier that one person's leisure is another's obligation, some other kayakers said that walking their dog was not something they did for fun. A second group of somewhat less common casual leisure interests was composed of reading and sending e-mail messages, watching films and videos, listening to music, surfing the Internet, and cycling around town. On average the sample spent slightly over an hour and a half each day at these activities, somewhat less than the average for the climbers. Note that, with all three samples, such averages hide the fact that, given the tendency to pursue these hobbies on weekends, there is rather less free time for casual leisure then than during the weekdays, as is left over after carrying out work and nonwork obligations.

As with the climbers the kayakers most often viewed casual leisure as a time for rest from physically or mentally demanding activity as well as for relaxation, during which a person might occasionally contemplate and daydream. A male kayaker, a teacher by vocation, held that casual leisure is,

> Fairly important, because most of the time I need to do something after work, because work dealing with the public is fairly stressful for me. It is more stressful than any sort of physical job. So I need something to wind down with; I need quiet time away from people. Whether it is working on the computer or reading, definitely . . . I will watch TV after school or after supper. . . . That is two different worlds, the school world and here. Here it is outside, outside, outside. . . . I'd say that, for stress relief, it is pretty important for me to do some sort of casual activity like that. Otherwise the days seem to collapse.

Slightly fewer kayakers brought up the balance question: the need to arrive in everyday life at an agreeable measure of the casual and the serious. For the large majority of respondents in this study, the serious element remains at center stage of their overall leisure lifestyle, but the casual element nevertheless plays a critical supporting role with reference to it.

> I don't allocate time. If not doing a serious leisure pursuit, then I will do casual leisure. Casual leisure is to pad time. I need the right balance, but it falls after serious leisure. How important? It is important, definitely, because I can't do serious leisure all the time. For example, last Sunday I could have paddled, but decided not to. Instead, I did personal errands and watched a movie. . . . And I'd say the socializing part of serious leisure is casual leisure for me, as well. – *male kayaker*

A female kayaker found balance through relaxation, in this way blending casual and serious leisure in her free-time, which, like that of the other kayakers, is dominated by serious leisure.

> I think it is important because it provides a balance. I can't kayak all the time, and it is just not physically possible to get myself to the river every single day. These casual things are convenient, and they don't demand

as much from me, mentally or physically, as kayaking does. And some of those are result oriented. In sewing and cooking I get to eat from the cooking. Walking the dog is particularly necessary, but it is more relaxing. Kayaking is not as relaxing as these other things are; it is nice to have the combination. I don't think I could kayak every single day, it would be too much, although I love it. I could try, that would be fun, but certainly not at the level that I play at. Say I was a kayaking instructor, it would be at a different level. I would be paddling at a different level than when I am out for my own pleasure. And that is what I do now, I paddle hard, I am challenging myself all the time. I wouldn't be doing that if I was teaching, if that was my job.

Here, too, a small percentage of the sample saw casual leisure as simply unimportant. As one male kayaker put it: "[it is] very unimportant. I don't need it to get through the day. It doesn't give me the satisfaction and gratification I look for in life. I could do without it." Yet doing without it can have deleterious consequences, among them burnout. Though it probably happens rather rarely, it is nonetheless possible to get burned out pursuing serious leisure, just as it is in some other, usually work-related, obligations.

In '98 I paddled lots and taught a lot. I worked night shifts to free time for my competing skills. By winter I was burnt out. Then Peter [pseudonym] and I went to Ecuador for one and a half months of paddling. It was trickier than rodeo. There were rough trees, and I got beyond where I should have been in a rodeo boat. It was continuous Class V, and I got pretty beat up, which set me back about two weeks. I needed time off to evaluate why I was paddling. It had gotten to the point where it wasn't fun, and I don't want to always push and be ompetitive. I had made the rodeo team and was supposed to do the rodeo circuit, but after Ecuador, I decided to take a break. I was burnt out. I took a year and a half off in '99. — *female kayaker*

In kayaking, too, balancing serious and casual leisure fails to show any differences along lines of gender or skill and experience.

Casual Leisure: Snowboarders

The principal casual leisure of the snowboarders is reading, socializing, watching films and videos, and watching television. Here, too, socializing, in its many different expressions, reigns supreme. By contrast, tending to the e-mail and walking a dog were, for this sample, the least popular. And, of the three groups, the snowboarders reported by far the largest average amount of daily time devoted to casual leisure: 3.5 hours. In good part this exceptional figure can be explained by the fact that, compared with the kayakers and climbers, many of them held part-time jobs or were unemployed, leaving thereby significantly more time for leisure of both kinds.

As for the meaning of casual leisure, the snowboarders were much in tune with the other two groups. The majority of them commented on its capacity to provide mental and physical rest in addition to relaxation. In the words of a female snowboarder:

> Rest on my body. That is a major thing. Often I just can't snowboard any more. I have got shin splints, which is a recurring injury that stops me snowboarding a lot. Just if you continually snowboard you get into a rut, you almost go backward. So I have found it is important to have a few days off, so that in the end, you are really desperate to get back out there and definitely go out for the motivation factor.

A male snowboarder had this to say about his casual leisure:

> I: *So you are looking at about fifteen hours a week. When you think about what it is you get from casual leisure, especially when you compare with what you get from serious leisure what is it that casual leisure gives you?*
>
> R: Just relaxation, just time to let your mind go numb.
>
> I: *And is that important?*
>
> R: Yeah, it figures to be for me. Everybody has got their way of doing it I guess. There is a lot of weed smokers, that is the way they kind of relax and do stuff. I have never been a video game player, so sitting on the couch more than anything just relaxing. Body needs time to rejuvenate, and I'm usually pretty much too tired to read.

A third, a male, recognized the possibility of burnout should he eschew casual leisure.

> Just to unwind it is important, for sure, 'cause you just don't want to burn yourself out. If you are going hard all the time, like during the day and at work and at night, then it won't take long and you get too burnt out. Then one thing will drop off, like. I find that, if I don't hang out at home and, like, do casual things, then my snowboarding will go down.

Although many fewer respondents mentioned it, use of free time for reflection – a form of casual leisure – was nevertheless recognized.

> Probably, like, a little personal reflection time I guess. If you are always doing with people you don't always get time to, like, think things out. 'Cause living here is totally like a bubble. You don't hear what happened on the news, you don't read the papers. Like you pretty much go with if it snowed or what is happening in the park or what your friends are doing on Friday. – *female snowboarder*

Only one respondent dwelt on the balance function of casual leisure, which he tied to both rest and relaxation.

> **I:** *Thinking now about what it is you get from casual leisure and what it is you get from serious leisure, how important is casual leisure to you and what does it offer you?*
>
> **R:** I think it is important, because you need a balance in your life. I think that it is really important for relaxing and just, like, renewing your energy, 'cause if you don't rest, your body won't function properly.
>
> **I:** *Is it all physical rest or is some of it mental rest as well?*
>
> **R:** It is hard to say, because mental rest, from what I have been saying throughout the whole thing, it [snowboarding] is not really very stressful mentally. Like, you are focused, and you are kind of in a different state of mind. When you stop at the end of the day or when you stop at the bottom of the hill, you are not really . . . I don't know. It is not really like stress; it is much more like exhilaration. – *male snowboarder*

And, as with the other two groups, a very small number of the snowboard sample qualified casual leisure as unimportant. "Not important," observed a male snowboarder. "It's zoning out by wasting time. I mope about. It's fill-in time." Further, only one respondent (female) in this sample noted the significance of casual leisure for expanding and maintaining a circle of friends that included people beyond the world of snowboarding.

> I: *So when you think about what it is you get from serious leisure and you also think about what it is that you get from casual leisure what does casual leisure give you that is different and how important is it to you?*

> R: Different because there is a lot of people I can hang around with that don't necessarily do the sports that I do. I am not such a person that, [for instance], because I climb I like climbers. Like I was saying before there are a lot of friends that I see outside of my leisure activities. Like Phil [pseudonym, boyfriend] doesn't climb or anything, but I still just get satisfaction of being with them basically and spending time with them that I don't necessarily. . . . Which is too bad: that I can't bring all my friends to do the things that I want to do. So I think you have to take time for everybody, which is really hard though. I go for supper with her, have a drink with her. I can't say no.

And, as earlier, there were no differences in gender, and skill and experience to help explain these patterns.

Toward an Optimal Leisure Lifestyle

I did not ask the interviewees in this study whether they regarded as optimal their leisure lifestyle. I reasoned that this question would be too abstract, and would result mostly in confused answers. Rather, I inferred optimization of leisure lifestyle from answers they gave to the three questions asked about their casual leisure and how it stood with reference to their serious leisure. The three inferences follow.

One, only a small minority of the respondents said they engaged in no casual leisure whatsoever, whereas the vast majority reported having a significant amount of it. I doubt that the leisure lifestyle of this minority could be qualified as optimal, for the three hobbies in question are both physically and mentally demanding. Even if a participant's life contained no disagreeable obligations, these hobbies cannot be pursued during all waking hours seven days a week. And it is highly unlikely that the participant's work is such that, to effectively serve there, no rest and relaxation beyond normal sleeping hours is required. That is, most work these days in Western society is not what I have referred to elsewhere as "devotee work" (Stebbins, 2004b), work that is as fulfilling as serious leisure itself and almost always a scion of it. What is more, as with serious leisure, devotee work also requires some time away from it.

Two, respondents with free time left over after they had engaged in their hobby appeared to have plenty of leisure alternatives to choose from that were both affordable and otherwise accessible. They seemed to be taking advantage of these at a rate and to the extent that could generate the level of enjoyment they were seeking. Moreover, these activities seemed to meet their desire to find rest and relaxation as well as balance between the serious and casual leisure sectors of their free time.

Three, all respondents had control over the amount of time they devoted to climbing, kayaking, and snowboarding *vis-à-vis* the amount they devoted to casual leisure. As just mentioned a few of them elected to devote no time whatsoever to the latter, and in their free time to exist instead on a steady diet of the former. But the rest had decided to strike a balance between serious and casual forms, based on the perceived complementarity of the two (in proper doses of each), and moreover, they were in a position to adjust this balance when they wanted to do so. At any given point in time, should the balance become unfavorable, they could, so far as free time is concerned, change it. What they often could not do was to change the amount of time devoted to work, so as to have more time for either serious or casual leisure. This does not affect optimal leisure lifestyle, nevertheless, for such a lifestyle is defined by the individual as ideal personal use of what free time is available, however little or much of that time there is.

My conclusion: a large majority of the overall sample have developed a truly optimal leisure lifestyle. In doing so, they have learned how to juggle their leisure activities, both serious and casual, in order to maintain this lifestyle. Nevertheless, in future research, we must strive to develop some direct measures of optimal leisure lifestyle, with the aim of producing more persuasive results than presented here on its nature and function in people's lives.

The Role of Work

Work for a large majority of the sample fills the function of being a livelihood. With it they are able to live at what they define as an acceptable level, while having enough free time for their casual and serious leisure. Work for most of this group is a means to an end, not an end in itself. To be sure, they try to minimize the disagreeableness of the job, as most everyone does, but if that job requires long hours and is tiring enough to leave little energy for the hobby, they would look for other employment. Most respondents in this study lived, presumably unwittingly, by Aristotle's dictum that "the end of labor is to gain leisure." Moreover, they have shown us some practical ways to achieve this goal in the twenty-first century.

Thus many members of the overall sample worked at what we might call "throwaway jobs," work relatively easily acquired and abandoned in harmony with important lifestyle goals of the individual employee. Those goals included, in this instance, finding an optimal leisure lifestyle. Working as janitor, short-order cook, store clerk, or restaurant server exemplify throwaway jobs. Other members of the sample worked, as it were, in the industry, as guides, instructors, maintenance workers, and the like. Some of this work is of the devotee variety, especially guiding and instructing, and as such, adds to the person's sense of fulfillment gained through both work and leisure. And, to be sure, it is not throwaway work.

Still others were employed in responsible, managerial, professional, or skilled labor or skilled service positions, also hardly work of the throwaway variety. Even then, some of this work was chosen with the hobby in mind; teaching, for instance, frees the teacher in summer for mountain climbing. Some of this work offers flexible hours, enabling more effective and frequent participation in the hobby.

Managerial, professional, and skilled labor and skilled service work generally pays better and is more prestigious than the throwaway job, and may even inspire occupational devotion. But, for this reason, the devotee occupations also tend to commit their employees to the job, and consequently truncate their options in free time. Many a respondent thus employed felt this pressure, and wished for more time for serious leisure. Even if they have developed an optimal leisure lifestyle, these people have yet to achieve an optimal general lifestyle, one composed of an agreeable blend of work, nonwork obligation, and leisure (casual and serious). In this regard, very few of the overall sample operated a retail or wholesale business, enterprises that commonly absorb a great deal of time.

On the whole, these hobbyists, intensely committed as they are to their leisure, have kept close watch on their work involvements, trying in whatever ways the involvements permit, to maximize free time. This has included for most, by the way, the decision to reside in Canmore rather than Calgary or another nearby community. Occupational choices are much more limited in the first and it can be a costly place to live, but it is closer to where they pursue their hobbies, and aesthetically more pleasing for the mountain enthusiast. Residing in Banff, it should be noted, is out of the question, unless in accordance with Parks Canada policy, the would-be resident is employed there in a way directly relating to either the town or the national park.

Voluntary Simplicity

To the extent these hobbyists have scaled down their employment aspirations to realize their free-time aspirations, we can say that they are giving expression to the principle of voluntary simplicity. In a book by the same title, Duane Elgin (1981) writes that, among other things, voluntary simplicity is a way of living that accepts responsibility for developing our human potential, as well as for contributing to the well-being of the world, of which we are an inseparable part. It involves a paring back of many, if not all, of the superficial aspects of our lives, so as to allow more time and energy for developing the heartfelt aspects of those lives. In brief, voluntary simplicity helps pave the road to self-fulfillment.

The voluntary simplicity movement, which also goes by the denominations of "simple living" and "creative simplicity," was launched in the mid-1930s with an article written by Richard Gregg (cited in Elgin, 1981, pp. 297-298). Since its adherents also espouse a variety of other principles, this way of living is by no means identical with the pursuit of serious leisure. Nevertheless, the two share the common ground of encouraging and fostering personal development through realizing individual human potential, while contributing to the development of the wider community.

These mountain hobbyists, as they personally advance in their activity, contribute to community by, among other ways, integrating individuals from diverse backgrounds into climbing and kayaking teams. That is, for a variety of reasons, the teams, if they are to function, must occasionally seek new members and people who, heretofore were strangers but have appropriate levels of skill and motivation, are usually welcome. All three hobbies also contribute to the community by offering fascinating displays of excellence in kayaking, snowboarding, and mountain climbing.

Voluntary simplicity, at whatever level of completeness it is sought, flies in the face of working and spending, both of which have been, for many years, the mantra of middle- and upper-class society in North America. To cut back on costs of housing, automotive transportation, consumer goods, and the like in order to save money, and with it, pursue serious leisure, is in this part of the world, a most unusual approach to free time. But the powerful appeal of serious leisure, the mountain hobbies included, demands this of participants of modest means. To be sure, such leisure has its own monetary costs in equipment and trips to distant slopes, rivers, and mountains, which force most people into some measure of frugality elsewhere in life. Moreover, engaging in such leisure generates a profound desire to do more of it more often, even if the time for this has to be taken from work.

It is not that the sample lives as paupers, even if some were living in quite small accommodations, eating and dressing simply, and getting around in an older car or truck than many other people in town. But most have compromised, in some significant way, their work hours, work schedule, work remuneration, or type of employment to facilitate pursuit of their serious leisure passions. In so doing they have, probably often without knowing it, shown their allegiance to the principle of voluntary simplicity. Just how voluntarily simplistic they are when it comes to buying equipment for their hobby is, however, another question.

I did not probe in the interviews on this matter, but I did get the sense that, generally, these hobbyists buy what they need at a level of quality necessary to get them effectively and efficiently through a typical outing at their level of competence. This is not being extravagant. Thus, a kayaker might own three different kinds of boats and routinely use all three, depending on the kind of water to be tackled and the sort of manoeuvres to be undertaken on it. Moreover, they will be of sufficient quality to effectively and efficiently enable this person to get the job done. Sure, using these standards, a few will be inclined to spend more than necessary, to buy the Cadillac of boats, for instance, when a Ford would do just as well. I once knew a cellist in a civic orchestra the quality of whose instrument would have inspired jealously in many a professional orchestral musician. But the cellist was eventually asked to leave the orchestra, because he was unable to play acceptably, according to the group's quite tolerant standards, even the simplest music that it presented at its concerts.

Conclusions:
Risk, Serious Leisure, and Quality of Life

We can learn something of lasting value from the hobbyists of this study, namely, that life can be enormously exciting, if only we would put ourselves in a position to experience serious leisure at a level of participation that generates such excitement. In activities like the nature-challenge hobbies, that excitement includes courting manageable risk in the search for flow, but seldom entering voluntarily into anything more hazardous than that. Still, a different challenge often emerges much earlier in the leisure career. For many people the first two steps leading to this state of excitement and fulfillment will be the most difficult: finding one or more serious leisure passions that can, in turn and where necessary, justify cutting back work hours and earned income to pursue them.

Indeed, even for those with sufficient free time and income to support their basic needs as well as their leisure interests, finding a deeply fulfilling pastime still presents a challenge all of its own. For the full range of serious leisure activities available to a particular person, taking account of age, sex, income, ability, aptitude, and geographic location, is rarely fully obvious to that person. Yet, with help of friends, relatives, lifestyle counsellors, specialized magazines, continuing education programs, and so on, would-be amateurs, hobbyists, and career volunteers should be able to find at least one activity into which they can throw themselves with enormous passion.

Serious leisure and quality of life have an obvious affinity for one another; as suggested in the old popular song "Love and Marriage," they go together like a horse and carriage (see the more detailed discussion of serious leisure and quality of life by Stebbins, 2005). Consider the want-based approach to quality of life, the approach used in this section. It consists of four components: "a sense of achievement in one's work, an appreciation of beauty in nature and the arts, a feeling of identification with one's community, a sense of fulfillment of one's potential" (Campbell, Converse, and Rogers, 1976, p. 1). This, a subjective approach, contrasts with the objective approach, which is founded on social indicators (see Markides, 1992); the former centers on people's perceptions, expectations, aspirations, and achievement orientations (Mukherjee, 1989, p. 44). Every serious leisure activity engenders at least three of the four components identified by Campbell and colleagues, with the arts and outdoor activities producing all four.

Where does quality of life fit in all this? Applying to leisure the first component – sense of achievement – it is evident from what was said earlier about the rewards of personal enrichment, self-expression, group accomplishment and contribution to the maintenance and development of the group as well as the characteristics of career, effort, benefits and perseverance that people can routinely find that sense here, and not just in a few lines of paid work. Successfully managing risk to experience flow, the stuff of the three mountain hobbies, is in these activities, clearly part of this sense. The second component, which refers to appreciation of beauty in nature and the arts, is as just noted, met in such serious leisure forms as the outdoor activities and artistic pursuits, including backpacking, cross-country skiing, sculpting, and playing string quartets.

Third, all serious leisure has links with the wider community, if in no other way, than through the social worlds of its participants. Additionally however, many serious leisure activities relate directly to the larger community through artistic performances by amateurs, interesting displays by hobbyists (of, for example, stamps, model trains, show dogs), and needed services by volunteers. Sense of fulfillment of one's potential – the fourth component – comes primarily from experiencing the reward of self-fulfillment, but also, to a lesser extent, from the serious leisure characteristics of finding a career in the activity and having to occasionally persevere at following it.

This close fit of serious leisure and quality of life gives substance to Neulinger's (1981, p. 66) observation that "leisure is not just a component of the quality of life, but the very essence of it. It is not a neutral state of mind, but a positive, highly desirable one, and an important value. Leisure in my opinion is the guideline needed for any decision relating to the quality of life." In other words, people find high quality of life, in part or in whole, through their serious leisure experiences. The nature-challenge hobbies considered in this book, with their dimension of manageable physical risk, are powerful evidence of that. These activities and others of the serious leisure genre give the lie to Horace's ancient and cynical comment that "we rarely find anyone who can say he has lived a happy life, and who, content with his life, can retire from the world like a satisfied guest."

Appendix
Interview Guide for Kayakers

The following is the final version of the interview guide for kayakers, the version that emerged over the course of the interviews. It is the product of the theoretical sampling that is such an essential part of exploratory research, which as the study progresses, results in numerous modifications in the interview guide. The interview guides used with the climbers and snowboarder were identical to this one, modified only where language required reference to the particular hobby.

I Career

A) Can you recall when you first became interested in kayaking? [describe how this happened]

B) How did this initial interest continue? [get history of involvement, including membership in clubs]

>1) Were any of your friends or relatives instrumental in your initial involvement in kayaking?

>2) Did you have any canoeing experience before you entered the world of kayaking?

C) Have you participated in any races in kayaking?

D) What thrills have you had in kayaking?

E) What disappointments have you had in kayaking?

F) What tensions are there in kayaking?

G) What are your plans for the future so far as kayaking is concerned?

II Lifestyle

A) How many hours would you estimate that you spend in a typical week during the season in kayaking, including volunteer work for the sport?

B) Are you a member of a kayak club or association (Y/N)?

C) On the average in the past season how many sessions of kayaking have you participated in each month?

D) What percentage of your close and moderately close friends and relatives are kayakers?

    1) Are your friends and relatives in kayaking mostly the same age as you?

III Family and Spouse or Other Companion

A) Does your companion (spouse, friend, etc.) accept, tolerate, or reject your   involvement in kayaking?

    1) (if he or she tolerates or rejects) What is there about the kayaking lifestyle that he or she dislikes?

B) Does your companion become involved in kayaking in any way?

C) Does the rest of your family become involved in kayaking in any way?

IV Work

A) What is your present job?

B) What is your present level of education?

C) Does your work conflict with kayaking?

    1) (if yes) How does work conflict?

D) Does work leave you fatigued for kayaking?

    1) Does kayaking leave you fatigued for work?

E) Is kayaking often on your mind at work?

V Orientations

A) What are the rewards of kayaking? [present to respondent card with list of rewards]

B) Major dislikes in kayaking [indicate that not interested in minor peeves]

C) Do you get nervous before races or challenging stretches of water?

     1) (if yes) How do you deal with it?

VI Casual Leisure

A) What casual leisure do you have in a typical week?

B) How much time do you think you spend doing casual leisure in a typical week?

C) Compared with your serious leisure how important is casual leisure to you and what does it offer you?

VII Miscellaneous

A) What are your other hobbies, avocations?

B) How old are you?

C) [note further observations and comments from respondent].

References

American Whitewater Association (2003). Rating scale. [http://www.awa.ord/safety/safety.html#rating scale].

Arai, S. M., & Pedlar, A.M. (1997). Building communities through leisure: Citizen participation in a healthy communities initiative. *Journal of Leisure Research*, 29(2), 167-182.

Baldwin, C. K., & Norris, Patricia A. (1999). Exploring the dimensions of serious leisure: `Love me--Love my dog!' *Journal of Leisure Research*, 31, 1-17.

Bourdieu, P. (1979). La distinction: Critique sociale du jugement. Paris : Les Editions de Minuit.

Bratton, R. D., Kinnear, G., & Koroluk, G. (1979). Why man climbs mountains. *International Review of Sport Sociology*, 14(2), 23-36.

Campbell, A., Converse, P., & Rogers, W.L. (1976). *The quality of American life: Perceptions, evaluations, and satisfactions.* New York: Russell Sage Foundation.

Campbell, J. B., Tyrell, D. J., & Zingaro, M. (1993). Sensation seeking among whitewater canoe and kayak paddlers. *Personality & Individual Differences*, 14(3), 489-491.

Celsi, R. L., Rose, R. L., & Leigh, T. W. (1993). An exploration of high-risk leisure consumption through sky-diving. *Journal of Consumer Research*, 20(1), 1-23.

Cnaan, R.A., Handy, F., & Wadsworth, M. (1996). Defining who is a volunteer: Conceptual and empirical considerations. *Nonprofit and Voluntary Sector Quarterly*, 25, 364-383.

Coakley, J. (2001). Sport in society: Issues and controversies, 7th ed. New York: McGraw-Hill.

Codina, N. (1999). Tendencias emergentes en el comportamiento de ocio: El ocio serio y su evaluacion. *Revista de Psicologia Social*, 14, 331-346.

Creyer, E.H., Ross, W.T., & Evers, D. (2003). Risky recreation: An exploration of factors influencing the likelihood of participation and the effects of experience. *Leisure Studies, 22,* 239-254.

Csikszentmihalyi, M. (1990). *Flow: The psychology of optimal experience.* New York, NY: Harper & Row.

Donnelly, P. (2004). Sport and risk culture. In K.E. Young (Ed.), *Sporting bodies, damaged selves: Sociological studies of sports-related injury.* Oxford, United Kingdom: Elsevier.

Dubin, R. (1992). *Central life interests: Creative individualism in a complex world.* New Brunswick, NJ: Transaction.

Economist (The) (1998). Winter wonderlands (29 January), 59.

———— (1999). Even campers grow old (9 September), 64.

———— (2001a). No room at the top: Congestion causing danger on the world's highest mountain (2 June), 39.

———— (2001b). Régine Cavagnoud. (17 November), 82.

Egner, H., Escher, A., Kleinhans, M., & Lindner, P. (1998). Extreme nature sports- spatial component of an active style of leisure pursuits. *Erde,* 129(2), 121-138.

Elgin, D. (1981). *Voluntary simplicity: Toward a way of life that is outwardly simple, inwardly rich.* New York: William Morrow.

Ewert A., & Hollenhorst, S. (1989). Testing the adventure model empirical support for a model of risk recreation participation. *Journal of Leisure Research,* 21(2), 124-139.

Fine, G. A. (1988). Dying for a laugh. *Western Folklore, 47,* 77-194.

Floro, G. K. (1978). What to look for in a study of the volunteer in the work world. In R. P. Wolensky, & Miller, E.J. (Ed.), *The small city and regional community* (pp. 194-202). Stevens Point, WI: Foundation Press.

Gibson, H., Willming, C., & Holdnak, A. (2002). We're gators . . . not just Gator fans: Serious leisure and University of Florida football. *Journal of Leisure Research,* 34(4), 397-425.

Glaser, B. G. (1978). *Theoretical sensitivity: Advances in the methodology of grounded theory.* Mill Valley, CA: Sociology Press.

Glaser, B. G., & Strauss, A.L. (1967). *The Discovery of grounded theory: Strategies for qualitative research.* Chicago, IL: Aldine Atherton.

Goffman, E. (1961). *Asylums : Essays on the social situation of mental patients and other inmates.* Chicago, IL: Aldine.

———— (1963). Stigma : *Notes on the management of spoiled identity.* Englewood Cliffs, NJ: Prentice Hall.

Griffiths, I. (1970). Gentlemen suppliers and with-it consumers. *International Review of Sport Sociology,* 5, 59-71.

Hall, P.M. (1987). Interactionism and the study of social organization. *The Sociological Quarterly,* 28, 1-22.

Harries, G. D., & Currie, R.R. (1998). Cognitive dissonance: A consequence of serious leisure. *World Leisure and Recreation,* 40(3), 36-41.

Heywood, I. (1994). Urgent dreams: Climbing, rationalization and ambivalence. *Leisure Studies,* 13, 179-194.

Humphreys, D. (1997). Shredheads go mainstream? Snowboarding and alternative youth. *International Review for the Sociology of Sport,* 32(2), 147-160.

International Canoe Federation (2003). History. [http://www.canoeicf.com/structure/history].

Jones, C.D., Hollenhorst, S.J., & Perna, F. (2003). An empirical comparison of the four channel flow model and adventure experience paradigm. *Leisure Sciences,* 25, 17-32.

Junger, S. (1999). *The perfect storm.* New York: Perennial.

Kiewa, J. (2002). Traditional climbing: Metaphor of resistance or metanarrative of oppression? *Leisure Studies,* 21(2), 145-162.

Kleiber, D.A. (2000) The neglect of relaxation. *Journal of Leisure Research,* 32, 82-86.

Krakauer, Jon (1997). *Into thin air.* Garden City, NY: Anchor.

Lee, Y., Datillo, J., & Howard, D. (1994). The complex and dynamic nature of leisure experience. *Journal of Leisure Research*, 26(3), 195.

Lipscomb, N. (1999). The relevance of the peak experience to continued skydiving participation: A qualitative approach to assessing motivations. *Leisure Studies*, 18, 267-288.

Lois, J. (2003). *Heroic efforts: The emotional culture of search and rescue volunteers*. New York: New York University Press.

Lyng, S. (1990). Edgework: A social psychological analysis of voluntary risk-taking. *American Journal of Sociology*, 95(4), 851-886.

Maines, D. R. (1982). In search of mesostructure. *Urban Life*, 11, 267-279.

Mannell, R. C. (1989). Leisure satisfaction. In E. L. Jackson & T. L. Burton (Ed.), *Understanding leisure and recreation: Mapping the past, charting the future* (pp. 281-301). State College, PA: Venture.

Mannell, R. C., & Kleiber, D.A. (1997). *A social psychology of leisure*. State College, PA: Venture.

Markides, K. (1992). Quality of life. In E. F. Borgatta &. M. L. Borgatta (Eds.), *Encyclopedia of sociology* (Vol. 3, pp. 1586-1595). New York: Macmillan.

Mckhann, M. (2001). Snowboarding. *Microsoft Encarta encyclopedia standard 2001*. (http://encarta.com)

Midol, N. (1993). Cultural dissents and technical innovations in the 'whiz' sports. International *Review for Sociology of Sport*, 28(1), 23-32.

Midol, N., & Broyer, G. (1995). Toward an anthropological analysis of new sport cultures: The case of whiz sports in France. *Sociology of Sport Journal*, 12(2), 204-212.

Mitchell, R. (1983). *Mountain experience: The psychology and sociology of adventure*. Chicago, IL: University of Chicago Press.

Mukherjee, R. (1989). *The quality of life valuation in social research*. New Delhi, India: Sage.

Nahrstedt, W. (2000). Global edutainment: The role of leisure education for community development. In A. Sivan & H. Ruskin (Eds.), *Leisure education, community development and populations with special needs* (pp. 65-74). Wallingford, Oxon, UK: CAB International.

Neulinger, J. (1981). *To leisure: An introduction.* Boston, MA: Allyn and Bacon.

Nixon, H. L, (1981), Birth order and preferences for risky sports among college students. *Journal of Sport Behavior,* 4(1), 12-23.

Pedersen, D. M. (1997). Perceptions of high-risk sports. *Perceptual and Motor Skills,* 85(2), 756-758.

Pociello, C. (1991). Concerning a few social functions of adventure. *Sociétés,* 34, 367-368.

Poole, E. (2003). Family mourns vibrant sisters. *Calgary Herald,* Wednesday 2 July, p. A1.

Robinson, D, W. (1985). Stress seeking: Selected behavioral characteristics. *Journal of Sport Psychology,* 7, 400-404.

Scott, C. (2000). *Pushing the limits: The story of Canadian mountaineering.* Calgary, AB: Rocky Mountain Books.

Shay, J. (1995). Achilles in Viet Nam. New York: Scribners.

Siegenthaler, K. L., & Gonzalez, G. L. (1997). Youth sports as serious leisure: A critique. *Journal of Sport & Social Issues,* 21(3), 298.

Slanger, E., & Rudestam, K. E. (1997). Motivation and disinhibition in high-risk sports: Sensation seeking and self-efficacy. *Journal of Research in Personality,* 31(3), 355-374.

Stebbins, R. A. (1979). *Amateurs: On the margin between work and leisure.* Beverly Hills, CA: Sage Publications.

Stebbins, R. A. (1992). *Amateurs, professionals and serious leisure.* Montreal, QC: McGill-Queen's University Press.

——— (1993). *Canadian football: The view from the helmet.* Toronto, ON: Canadian Scholars Press.

Stebbins, R. A. (1994). The liberal arts hobbies: A neglected subtype of serious leisure. *Loisir et societe/Society and leisure*, 17(1), 173-186.

—— (1996a). *The barbershop singer: Inside the social world of a musical hobby*. Toronto, ON: University of Toronto Press.

—— (1996b). Volunteering: A serious leisure perspective. *Nonprofit and Voluntary Sector Quarterly*, 25, 211-224.

—— (1997a). Casual leisure: A conceptual statement. *Leisure Studies*, 16(1), 17-25.

—— (1997b). Lifestyle as a generic concept in ethnographic research. *Quality and Quantity*, 31, 347-360.

—— (1998a). *The urban francophone volunteer: Searching for personal meaning and community growth in a linguistic minority*, Vol. 3 (2). Seattle, WA: Canadian Studies Center, University of Washington.

—— (1998b). *After work: The search for an optimal leisure lifestyle*. Calgary, AB: Detselig.

—— (2000a). Optimal leisure lifestyle: Combining serious and casual leisure for personal well-being. In M. C. Cabeza (Ed.), *Leisure and human development: Proposals for the 6th World Leisure Congress*. (pp. 101-107). Bilbao, Spain: University of Deusto.

—— (2000b). Obligation as an aspect of leisure experience. *Journal of Leisure Research*, 32, 152-155.

—— (2001a). *New directions in the theory and research of serious leisure*. Lewiston, New York: Edwin Mellen.

—— (2001b). *Exploratory research in the social sciences*. Thousand Oaks, CA: Sage.

—— (2001c). The costs and benefits of hedonism: Some consequences of taking casual leisure seriously. *Leisure Studies*, 20(4), 305-309.

Stebbins, R. A. (2001d). Volunteering – mainstream and marginal: Preserving the leisure experience. In M. G. M. Foley (Ed.), *Volunteering in leisure: Marginal or inclusive?* (Vol. 75, pp. 1-10). Eastbourne, UK: Leisure Studies Association.

————— (2002a). Choice in experiential definitions of leisure. *Leisure Studies Association Newsletter,* 63 (November), 18-20.

————— (2002b). *The organizational basis of leisure participation: A motivational exploration.* State College, PA: Venture Publishing.

————— (2004a). Introduction. In R. A. Stebbins, & M. M. Graham (Eds.), *Volunteering as leisure/leisure as volunteering: An international assessment* (pp. 1-12). Wallingford, Oxon, UK: CAB International.

————— (2004b). *Between work and leisure: The common ground of two separate worlds.* New Brunswick, NJ: Transaction Publishers.

————— (2005). Project-based leisure: Theoretical neglect of a common use of free time. *Leisure Studies,* 23 (3).

————— (2005). Project-based leisure: Theoretical neglect of a common use of free time. *Leisure Studies,* 24 (1), 1-11.

————— (in press). Serious leisure, volunteerism, and quality of life. In J. Haworth & T. Veal (Eds.), *The future of work and leisure.* London: Routledge.

Unruh, D. R. (1979). Characteristics and types of participation in social worlds. *Symbolic Interaction,* 2, 115-130.

————— (1980). The nature of social worlds. *Pacific Sociological Review,* 23, 271-296.

Vaske, J.J., Carothers, P., Donnelly, M.P., & Baird, B. (2000). Recreation conflict among skiers and snowboarders." *Leisure Sciences,* 22, 297-313.

Webster, E. (2001). Mountain climbing: History. Microsoft encarta encyclopedia standard 2001.

Williams, T., & Donnelly, P. (1985). Subcultural production, reproduction, and transformation in climbing. *International Review for the Sociology of Sport*, 20 (1/2), 3-16.

Zuzanek, J. (1996). Canada. In G. Cushman, A.J. Veal, & J. Zuzanek (Eds.), *World leisure participation: Free time in the global village* (pp. 35-76). Wallingford, Oxon, Eng.: CAB International.

Index

amateurs and amateurism, 30
    career (leisure) of, 66-69
    compared with hobbyists, 30
    and competition in skiing, 63
    and dedication, 45
    marginal nature of, 37
    social world of, 114
    See also serious leisure
Arai, S. M., 90

Baird, B., 147
Baldwin, C. K., 67
benefits, 33
    of casual leisure, 38-40
    durable, 33
    rewards, distinguished from, 35
Borgatta, E.F., 144
Borgatta, M.L., 144
Bourdieu, P., 24, 100, 115
Bratton, R, D., 21
Broyer, G., 14
Burton, T.L., 144

Cabeza, M.C., 146
Campbell, A., 135
Campbell, J.B., 21, 25
career (leisure), 67-88, 134
    and casual leisure, 38
    definition of, 67
    future of, 86-87
    and gender, 73, 75, 76
    kayaking, 70-71, 73-75, 86-78
    and lifestyle, 23-24, 43
    as mesostructure, 8
    mountain climbing, 69, 72-73, 86

    nature-challenge hobbies and, 65, 67-88
    and organizations, 67-68
    and rewards, 36
    and role, 33
    and serious leisure, 29, 32, 33
    snowboarding, 69-70, 71, 75-77, 87
    stages of, 68-69, 69-77, 87-88, 134
    and thrills, 77-86
Carothers, P., 147
casual leisure, 37-40
    benefits of, 33, 38-40
    and career, 38
    of climbers, 120-123
    definition of, 29
    as "edutainment," 39
    and gender differences, 123, 125
    helping as, 32
    and identity, 35
    and interpersonal relationships, 39-40
    of kayakers, 123-125
    and leisure lifestyle, 43
    and optimal leisure lifestyle, 40, 44, 128-130
    as relaxation, 37, 39, 121, 124, 126, 129
    and regeneration, 39
    and serendipity, 38
    of snowboarders, 126-128
    and social world, 113
    types of 37-38
    as unimportant, 125, 127
    and well-being 40
    See also flow
Celsi, R. L., 21

central life interest, 45-46
  definition of, 45
  and identity, 23, 45-46
  and serious leisure, 45, 46
challenging nature, 9, 65
  concept of, 7
  as hobby, 15-22, 25-26, 31
  as manageable challenge, 17, 21
  motivation to engage in, 8
  as sport, 16, 47
  See also mountain climbing; kayaking; snowboarding
choice of leisure, 31
climbing walls, 52
Cnaan, R.A., 31
Coakley, J., 16
Codina, N., 92
commitment, 37
  and career stage, 77
  and core activity, 25
  and thrills, 77-78
Converse, P., 135
core activity (tasks), 15-16, 22
  and commitment, 25
  of kayaking, 16, 54-56, 58
  of mountaineering, 16, 48-49, 53-54
  of snowboarding, 16, 60, 61, 64
  costs, 9, 25, 9, 101-102
  as disappointments, 95-97
  as dislikes, 100-101
  in nature challenge hobbies, 95-101
  in optimal leisure lifestyle, 44
  and rewards, 35, 90
  rewards, as counterweights to, 35, 90
  in serious leisure, 92, 95-101, 101-102

  as tensions, 97-100
  types of, 35, 95-101
Creyer, E.H., 21
Csikszentmihalyi, M., 16, 40-41
culture. *See* subculture
Currie, R.R., 92
Cushman, G., 148

Datillo, J., 144
devotee work, 40, 111, 129, 130, 131
devotees and participants, 24-25, 30,
  definition of 24
  in social worlds, 114-115
disappointments. *See* costs
dislikes. *See* costs
distinction (Bourdieu), 24, 100,
  and social world, 115
Donnelly, M.P., 25
Donnelly, P., 18, 148
Dubin, R., 23, 45-46

edgework, 14, 21
edutainment, 39
Egner, H., 14
Elgin, D., 131-132
epics, 81-86
  definition of, 80
Escher, A., 142
Evers, D., 21, 142
Ewert, A., 25

family, 9,
  and career (leisure), 24
  lifestyle dimension in, 103, 105-108
Fine, G. A., 33

Floro, G.K., 33
flow, 16-18, 20, 40-42, 47
    and devotee work, 40
    in kayaking, 94, 134, 135
    in mountain climbing, 134, 135
    as reward, 40
    and risk, 94
    and sensation seeking, 21
    and serious leisure, 40, 42
    in snowboarding, 134, 135
Foley, M.G.M., 147
fulfillment. *See* self-fulfillment

gender, 128
    in kayaking, 73, 75, 99, 107, 125
    iin mountain climbing, 70, 78
    in snowboarding, 76, 78, 105, 128
Gibson, H., 33
Glaser, B.G., 27, 28
Goffman, E., 37
Graham, M.M., 147
Griffiths, I., 14

Hall, P.M., 22
Handy, F., 31
Harries, G.D., 92
Haworth, J., 147
Heywood, I., 49
hobby,
    as activity participation, 28
    career in a, 24, 67-88
    challenging nature as, 65
    and competition, 31, 65
    as serious leisure, 29
    social world of, 113-116
    subculture of, 115-116

    and work, 110, 112, 130-131
    See also rewards; hobbyists and hobbyism; project-based leisure; serious leisure
hobbyists and hobbyism,
    definition of, 30
    as devotee, 24-25
    as mesostructural phenomena, 21-22, 115
    motivation in 16
    as participant, 25-25
    as sport participant, 16
    types of, 30-31
    and voluntary simplicity, 131-134
    and work, 130-131
    See also hobby; project-based leisure; serious leisure
Holdnak, A., 33
Hollenhorst, S.J., 21, 25
Howard, D., 92

ice climber. *See* mountain/ice climber
ice climbing, 49,
    See also mountain/ice climbing
identity, 20
    and central life interest, 23, 45-46
    and lifestyle, 43
    and serious leisure, 35
    and work, 108-113
indoor climbing. See climbing walls

Jackson, E.L., 144
Jones, C.D., 21
Junger, S., 20

kayakers
    age of, 26
    casual leisure of, 123-126, 129
    friends/relatives of, 104-105
    lifestyle (leisure) of, 104-105,
    106-107, 109-111, 116-117
    marital status of, 107
    occupational/educational status
    of, 109
    optimal leisure lifestyle of,
    128-130
    organizational membership,
    63, 104
    sex of, 26
    and voluntary simplicity, 132-
    134
    as volunteers, 117
    See also kayaking
kayaking,
    careers (leisure) in, 70-71, 73-
    75, 78-80, 87
    as central life interest, 111
    classes of difficulty, 58-59
    costs of, 96-97, 98-99, 101
    family and, 106-107
    flow and, 42, 94
    and fulfillment, 16-17
    history of, 56-60
    market appeal of, 47
    as nature-challenge hobby, 15-
    22, 47, 65
    organizations in, 57, 59, 63,
    104,
    rewards of, 94-95
    and risk, 21, 86
    season, 104
    social world of, 113-116
    as sport, 15, 59-60, 65
    spouse's reaction, 106
    technological advances in, 47
    thrills in, 78-80
    and work, 109-111,. 130-131

    See also kayakers, gender in
    kayaking
kayaks and paddles, 54-55
    uses of, 55-56
Kiewa, J. 50
Kinnear, G., 21
Kleiber, D.A., 39, 89
Kleinhans, M., 142
Koroluk, G, 21
Krakauer, J., 20

Lee, Y., 92
Leigh, T. W., 21
lifestyle (leisure), 103-113, 116-
    117
    activity dimension of, 104-105
    family dimension of, 103, 105-
    108
    and identity, 43
    of kayaking, 104-105, 106-
    107, 109-111, 116-117
    of mountain climbing, 104,
    105-107,108-109, 116-117
    organizations and, 44
    of snowboarding, 105, 107-
    108, 112-113, 116-117
    work dimension of, 108-113
    See also optimal leisure lifestyle
Lindner, P., 142
Lipscomb, N., 21
Lois, J., 20
Lyng, S., 8, 13, 14, 21

Maines, D.R., 8, 22
manageable challenge (risk), 17,
    21, 134, 136
Mannell, R.C., 89
Markides, K., 135
Mckhann, K., 62

mesostructure, 8, 22
 definition of, 22
 See also lifestyle (leisure); social
 world
Midol, N., 14
Miller, E.J., 142
Mitchell, R., 25, 50
motivation,
 and career, 88
 and costs, 25, 92, 95-101
 and flow, 42
 and fulfillment, 35, 101
 and lifestyle (leisure), 102
 and nature-challenge hobbies,
 8, 9, 25
 psychology of, 89-90, 101-102
 rewards and, 90-92, 92-95
 and social world, 102
mountain/ice climbers
 age of, 26
 casual leisure of, 120-123
 friends/relatives of, 104
 lifestyle (leisure) of, 104, 105-
 107,108-109, 116-117
 marital status of, 105
 occupational/educational status
 of, 108
 optimal leisure lifestyle of,
 128-130
 organizational involvement of,
 104
 sex of, 26
 and voluntary simplicity, 132-
 134
 as volunteers, 117
 See also gender in mountain
 climbing; mountain/ice climbing
mountain/ice climbing,
 careers (leisure) in, 65, 69, 70,
 72-73, 86

classes of difficulty, 53-54
 clubs in, 53
 costs of, 96, 97-98, 100-101
 epics in 81-85
 family and, 105-106
 and flow, 41, 94
 and fulfillment, 16-17
 history of, 50-54
 market appeal of, 47
 mountaineering as, 50-54
 as nature-challenge hobby, 7,
 15-22, 47, 65
 nature of, 48
 rewards of, 92-93
 and risk, 13, 21, 49-50, 94
 season of, 104
 social world of, 113-116
 as sport, 48-49, 52-53
 thrills in, 78
 types of, 48-49
 and work, 108-109, 130-131
 See also climbing walls, rock
 climbing
mountaineering. See mountain/ice
 climbing
mountaineers. See mountain/ice
 climbers
mountain hobby culture. See subculture
Mukherjee, R., 135

Nahrstedt, W., 39
nature challenge. See challenging
 nature
nature challenge hobby. See challenging nature, as hobby
Neulinger, J., 136
Nixon, H.L., 14
Norris, P. A., 67

obligation, 29, 123
    in optimal leisure lifestyle, 131
    in volunteering, 31
optimal leisure lifestyle, 9, 44, 119-136
definition of, 40
    and self-fulfillment, 9
    See also lifestyle

P-A-P system, 30
participants. *See* devotees and participants
Pedersen, D.M., 13
Pedlar, A.M., 90
Perna, F., 21
Pociello, C., 25
Poole, C., 19

quality of life, 9, 134-136
    and optimal leisure lifestyle, 40, 44
    and serious leisure, 134-136

rewards,
    and costs, 35
    definition of 36
    and durable benefits, 35
    and gender differences, 102
    and level of experience, 102
    and motivation, 90
    and quality of life, 135
    and self-fulfillment, 101
    of serious leisure, 35-37
    studying, 91-92
    as thrills, 77-78
risk,
    abhorred, 13
    as edgework, 14
    and flow, 16-18, 94, 135
    fortuitous high, 18-19, 85

high, 13-15, 16, 17
humanitarian high, 20-21
in kayaking, 21, 86
low (improbable), 14, 15
manageable, 17, 78, 134, 135, 136
in mountain climbing, 13, 49-50, 94
in nature-challenge hobbies, 8, 15
perceived, 17-18, 86
seeking as leisure, 8, 14-15
seeking as motive, 8, 22
and self-fulfillment, 8
sense of, 17-18
in snowboarding,
social high, 19-20
and subculture (mountain), 7, 115-116
unmanaged high, 18
voluntary, 8, 13
Robinson, D.W., 21
rock climbing, 49
    as flow, 41
    as high risk, 13
    indoor, 52
    as single pitch mountain climbing, 49
Rogers, W.L., 135
Rose, R. L., 21
Ross, W.T., 21
Rudestam, K.E., 14
Ruskin, H., 145

Scott, C., 48, 51
scrambling, 48
    definition of, 48, 54
    and flow, 42
    self-fulfillment, 8,
    and central life interest, 45
    and disappointment, 95, 96

in epics, 90
through kayaking, 65, 73
and motivation, 89-90, 101
through mountain climbing, 65
in nature challenge hobbies, 16-17
and optimal leisure lifestyle, 9, 119
and quality of life, 134-135
as reward, 90, 91, 92, 94, 95
through snowboarding, 60, 65, 95
and voluntary simplicity, 132
and work, 108-113, 129, 130
serious leisure, 29, 30-37
and career (leisure), 29, 67-88
and central life interest, 45-46
choice and, 31
as civil labor, 42
and the community, 37, 135
definition of, 29
distinguishing qualities, 33-35
and flow, 41
and identity, 35, 45-46
and lifestyle (leisure), 43, 103-113
marginality of, 37
motivation to engage in, 89-102
as nature challenge, 17
and optimal leisure lifestyle, 40, 44, 119-136
and P-A-P system, 30
and quality of life, 134-136
rewards of, 35-37
risk in, 8, 134
social world and, 34, 113-116
types of, 30-32
and voluntary simplicity, 131-134

See also amateurs and amateurism; hobbyists and hobbyism; volunteers and volunteering
Shay, J., 20
shoptalk, 85
Sivan, A., 145
Slanger, E., 14
snowboarders,
    age of, 26
    casual leisure of, 126-128
    friends/relatives of, 105
    lifestyle (leisure) of, 105, 107-108, 112-113, 116-117
    marital status of, 107
    occupational/educational status of, 112
    optimal leisure lifestyle of, 128-130
    sex of, 26
    and voluntary simplicity, 132-134
    as volunteers, 117
    See also gender in snowboarding; snowboarding
snowboarding,
    careers (leisure) in, 65, 71, 75-77, 87
    classes of difficulty, 64-65
    costs of, 97, 99-100,
    epics in, 81
    family and, 107-108
    history of, 62-65
    as nature challenge hobby, 15
    nature of, 60-61
    organizations in, 105
    rewards of, 95
    and risk, 21, 64
    season of, 105
    social world of, 113-116
    as sport, 47, 63-65

thrills in, 80-81
  See also snowboarders
snowboards, 60, 61-62
social world, 113-116
  definition of, 34
  as distinguishing quality of
  serious leisure, 34
  and project-based leisure, 42
  as reward in serious leisure, 36
  and subculture, 115-116
  types of members, 113-115
Stebbins, R.A., 23, 24, 28, 29-46,
  46, 69, 90, 111, 116, 129,
Strauss, A.L., 28
study design, 9, 23-28
subculture, 115-116
  mountain hobby culture, 7

tensions. *See* costs
thrills, 77-86
  definition of 77
  as epics, 81-86
  in kayaking, 78-80
  in mountain climbing, 78
  as rewards, 77-78
  in snowboarding, 80-81
Tyrell, D. J., 141

Unruh, D.R., 23, 34, 113, 115

Vaske, J.J., 100
Veal, A.J., 147, 148
voluntary simplicity, 131-134
volunteers and volunteering, 31-32
  career and, 68
  as casual leisure (casual volunteering), 32, 38
  and central life interest, 46

and conflict with nature challenge hobbies, 117
definition of, 31
peak, 20-21
as project-based leisure, 42,
117
and quality of life, 134-135
rewards of, 36-37, 98-99
as serious leisure, 30, 31-32
types of organizational, 32
See also serious leisure; casual
  leisure, project-based leisure

Wadsworth, M., 31
Webster, E., 52
Williams, T., 25
Willming, C., 33
Wolensky, R.P., 142
Work,
  and career, 67
  and casual leisure, 121, 124
  as central life interest, 45-46
  devotee, 111
  and leisure, 72, 94, 133, 134
  lifestyle dimension in, 108-113
  importance of, 130-131
  and optimal leisure lifestyle, 43
  and quality of life, 135

Young, K.E., 142

Zingaro, M., 21, 25
Zuzanek. J., 148